Writing Through the Year

winter spring summer autumn

Winslow Eliot

WRITING THROUGH THE YEAR (The Four Seasons)

Cover Designed by: Telemachus Press, LLC

Cover Art :
Copyright © thinkstockphotos/109185220
Copyright © thinkstockphotos/109185205
Copyright © thinkstockphotos/109185211
Copyright © thinkstockphotos/96012249

Published by: Telemachus Press, LLC
http://www.telemachuspress.com

Visit the author website:
http://www.winsloweliot.com

ISBNs:
978-1-938701-91-7 (eBook)
978-1-938701-92-4 (Paperback)
978-1-938701-93-1 (Workbook)

978-1-937698-85-0 (*Winter*)
978-1-937698-86-7 (*Spring*)
978-1-937698-87-4 (*Summer*)
978-1-937698-88-1 (*Fall*)

Version 2012.11

Acknowledgements

This book wouldn't exist without my publisher, Claudia Jackson, who gave me the concept, production, covers, and ongoing advice and encouragement. Thank you from the bottom of my heart! Also, gratitude to Nancy Crompton, May Paddock, and Samantha Stier, who were invaluable through the editing process. Thanks most of all to my visitors to the Write Spa over the years: the many readers and subscribers who have given me feedback, commented, supported, critiqued, appreciated, and were refreshed and rejuvenated by their pause at this oasis.

Table of Contents

Spring

APRIL

Week 14—Spring gets in your eyes
Week 15—Assonance
Week 16—Never be inhospitable to strangers
Week 17—Kisses

MAY

Week 18—Elemental beings
Week 19—Nonsense makes us smarter
Week 20—What is your internal age?
Week 21—The nose knows

JUNE

Week 22—Why I dance
Week 23—Men and women
Week 24—Sitting is deadly
Week 25—Satisfying conclusions
Week 26—Letting go

Summer

JULY

Week 27—Stream of consciousness
Week 28—Do nothing
Week 29—Why I love fiction
Week 30—There are no words for it

AUGUST

Week 31—Let me love you
Week 32—Writing slowly
Week 33—Message in a bottle
Week 34—Napping makes you smarter

SEPTEMBER

Week 35—A place of your own
Week 36—Castling, forking, and making luft
Week 37—Ask yourself: "Is this vital?"
Week 38—Show don't tell
Week 39—Surprise!

Autumn

OCTOBER

Week 40 — Be your own teacher
Week 41 — Transitions
Week 42 — Ghost story
Week 43 — Murder your darlings

NOVEMBER

Week 44 — Nyai Loro Kidul
Week 45 — Creating a poem
Week 46 — What makes people laugh?
Week 47 — Thanksgiving

DECEMBER

Week 48 — Does it matter?
Week 49 — Observation
Week 50 — Three wishes
Week 51 — Pictures, scissors, glue
Week 52 — Janusian thinking

Preface

Your life is an adventure. Every morning you wake up and anything at all might happen! You can set off on a journey, speak your mind, buy something, sell something, look at a painting, take a walk and see a wild boar … the possibilities are endless.

As a writer, you know this is true. You create worlds with the soul of an adventurer. You create things—you cast a magic spell and a world is manifested. A person is developed. A story unfolds.

The adventure is thrilling—but it can take its toll. Rest, pleasure, enjoyment in the journey is as important as charging into the fray. You need an oasis.

The oasis I offer you here is designed to rejuvenate and encourage you. It's supposed to be fun, fulfilling, and to inspire serenity and nourishment for your writer's soul.

Perhaps you write because you've been struck by a thunderbolt of inspiration. Or you're under deadline. Or you're trying to make money as a writer. Or you write because you enjoy it. Any of these reasons may create a stormy relationship with Writing. But your decision to write is a commitment as important as marriage. Writing needs nurturing, sustenance, and daily practice. Deadlines and inspiration don't cut it, just as they don't in a relationship. A pianist practices every day. A painter sketches every day. A lover pays tender attention to the beloved every day.

When I realized this, I decided I would give Writing all the honor and affection it was due, and see if I could lift it into a daily practice that brought us pleasure and joy.

In the years that followed this decision I've discovered that Writing is not something to wrestle with, or long for, or something that makes me giddy with excitement, or throws me into the bleakest despair imaginable. It's actually something that is always there for me, and I am always there for it. Since I began writing as a daily practice, our bond has become indissoluble.

My hope is that the exercises, insights, and encouragement I offer here will nourish and revitalize your own relationship with Writing.

You may be able to take a break from writing, but you won't be able to take a break from being a writer. –Stephen Leigh

Introduction

Writing is an adventure. -Winston Churchill

HOW TO MAKE THIS BOOK YOUR OWN

Your goal in allowing these practices into your life is pleasure and fun. Think of them as a spa—a restful massage, a pedicure that leaves your toenails polished and sparkling, and your writing muscles relaxed and flexible. They are designed to inspire, to relax, and to enjoy.

The book is divided into four parts: Winter, Spring, Summer, and Autumn. You'll find a writing practice for every week of the year so you can focus on each of the restful and rejuvenating practices for at least seven days. I've given each month four weeks, and one extra week for each of the four seasons, so that ultimately your writing adventure will cover an entire year. But it's important for you to keep in mind that you need to decide what works best for you. If you're working on developing your awareness of color, for example, then by all means continue with that practice for as long as you like.

Keep in mind that the 'in-between' moments of writing are as essential as the actual process of putting words together to create sentences. Just as white space is crucial in a design, and the rests between notes of music are as important as the notes themselves, so it is with the process of writing.

Become aware that everything you 'do' is writing.

Exercise the writing muscle every day, even if it is only a letter, notes, a title list, a character sketch, a journal entry. Writers are like dancers, like athletes. Without that exercise, the muscles seize up. –Jane Yolen

Writing Practices

Each practice begins with a musing that has some relevance to the practice. This helps get you in the mood, makes you think, or gives you a background to why this particular practice will help.

Set yourself a regular time each day to read the practice. You'll find that some of them aren't necessarily physical writing, but napping, taking a walk, or meditating… Every practice, however, feeds your writing soul.

When you're in any relationship, you experience situations or moments when you're frustrated or annoyed, there are always ups and downs. If the relationship is strong, eventually you move past those feelings into camaraderie and enjoyment in each other's company. That's what falling in love with Writing is like.

You'll find, if you follow a weekly rhythm as faithfully as possible, that by the end of the year you will have created a relationship with Writing that isn't anguished, tense, hard-working, or anxious, but instead has evolved into one that's filled with delight, fun, humor, meaning, and love.

Some of my favorite stories to read are from the Thousand-and-One Arabian Nights. The sense of adventure, the enticing smells and sounds of a Persian bazaar, the strums from the ouds, the fragrant spices, the romance, the desert, the music, the waterfalls—all these images carry me to a world where I am boundless, thrilled, myself. Just as we all have our own age, we all have a place where we feel at home, even if we've never been there. I've met people who aspire to climb high mountains, others who seek to journey through tropical jungles, others who feel passion for old Scottish castles. What's your dream? From your inward wanderings you explore even more aspects and attributes of yourself.

When you write, use all your senses. Include all its opulence, dreaminess, exotic, fairy-tale qualities of the place you're in. Imagine rare silks and velvets, a sky thick with stars, secret gardens. Maybe you have a small glass bottle of the essential oils of rosewood, jasmine, ylang ylang, amber, sandalwood, musk. Open it: breathe the fragrance deep.

Words are the genie in the bottle. They are magic. And magic creates something: a flying carpet, a fabulous dinner, a friend, a journey. All these things are created out of the magic of writing.

Just as evocative aromas can be used to heal or invigorate or inspire, so can writing. Imagine the words, open them, mix them, place them, breathe them. The ideas, whether they emerge from the exquisite glass bottle as a frustrated imp or a spirit of profundity, are freed. Let them do their own work.

Remember to use much more than visual imagery: evoke all your senses—the feel of rain on your face, the sound of a seagull crying, the taste of fear, the scent of orange blossoms.

Enjoy the process—the words—the sentences—the emotional rollercoaster—the satisfaction of nourishing your writing soul and heart. Enjoy just being together.

There is no satisfactory explanation of style, no infallible guide to good writing, no assurance that a person who thinks clearly will be able to write clearly, no key that unlocks the door, no inflexible rules by which the young writer may steer his course. He will often find himself steering by stars that are disturbingly in motion. -E. B. White

<u>*What are Daily Happinesses?*</u>

Throughout your WriteSpa you'll come across "daily happinesses." These are brief images or feelings that help you to peek into another, more objective, reality.

In a way, they are also writing prompts. Each one of these little phrases conjures a vignette, a mood, a story, a person, a place. For example: "Planning for a garden of rare and wild roses." "Penguins diving into the sea." "The silence before applause."

Let me explain further.

When I was in college back in the seventies, I came across this paragraph, written by Sylvia Plath in *Johnny Panic and the Bible of Dreams*:

> *"How I envy the novelist! I imagine her… pruning a rosebush with a large pair of shears, adjusting her spectacles, shuffling about among teacups, humming, arranging ashtrays or babies, absorbing a slant of light, a fresh edge to the weather, and piercing, with a kind of modest, beautiful x-ray vision, the psychic interiors of her neighbors – her neighbors on trains, in the dentist's waiting room, in the corner teashop. To her, this fortunate one, what is there that isn't relevant! Old shoes can be used, doorknobs, air letters, flannel nightgowns, cathedrals, nail varnish, jet planes, rose arbors, and budgerigars; little mannerisms – the sucking at a tooth, the tugging at a hemline – any weird or warty or fine or despicable thing. Not to mention emotions, motivations – those rumbling, thunderous shapes. Her business is Time, the way it shoots forward, shunts back, blooms, decays, and double-exposes itself. Her business is people in Time. And she, it seems to me, has all time in the world. She can take a century if she likes, a generation, a whole summer. I can take about a minute."*

For me, reading this paragraph was a revelation. Writing furiously at the time, both novels and poetry, I knew in an instant what she meant. Every single detail in life – doorknobs, the tugging at a hemline – is relevant to a novelist. This makes daily life even more enticing and appealing.

Daily happinesses are more than just writing prompts to get you started. They each morph into a small awareness that keeps you alive to the subtle qualities of writing fiction. Just as on the stage of a play, every prop is relevant to the action, characters, and dialog, so every detail in a story is relevant. It matters.

It also inspires.

So come up with your own, as often as possible, but at least once a day. Simply observe the folded sheets, or the curled-up cat, or the sleet at the window, or the quirky smile of a friend, and write it down. You might be amazed at the story that surrounds an everyday image when seen in a different light.

Now… enjoy the writing journey. And remember that rest is as important as movement.

Most people would rather be certain they're miserable, than risk being happy.

-Robert Anthony

WriteSpa

Writing through the year . . .

January

Week 1 – Hypnopompia: your best time to "write"
Week 2 – When you read about a new hat, why do you want one too?
Week 3 – The art of meditation
Week 4 – Know thyself: Use the craft of interviewing to find out more about you

WEEK 1

Consciousness: that annoying time between naps. -Author Unknown

Hypnopompia—your best time to write

Hypnopompia is that marvelous in-between moment before you're fully awake. Hypnagogia, which also works, is the state just before you fall asleep. Either way, it's the time when you'll find you do your best work. Many scientists and artists used this time to access inspiration, including Aristotle, Thomas Edison, Albert Einstein, and Salvador Dali. It's when, as a writer, you'll have your greatest insights.

Remember, the act of writing is not just about putting your pen to paper or your fingers to the keyboard. It's also about daydreaming, making up stories, reading, and thinking about words: their meaning and their sacredness, their value to you as a writer, and their kindness and helpfulness.

Regard this state as a sacred trust. It's a flame, a fire, warmth—an inspiring way to think outside the box. It helps you to look at something freshly and strangely. This is the time to let an image or a phrase come to you, instead of always being the one to search for it.

A study in the Journal for Neuropathy reports a correlation between hypnogogia and the enhancement of creative ability. In the study, creativity was defined by: "(a) fluency (the ability to generate numerous ideas), (b) flexibility (the ability to see a given problem from multiple perspectives), and (c) originality (the ability to come up with new and unique ideas)." Although fluency did not significantly increase, flexibility in thinking and well-being increased for everyone.

During hypnagogia, the normal activity of the left / logical side of your brain is inhibited, allowing imagery in your right / creative brain freedom to experience whatever it wants to, without trying to analyze itself. Often what you experience may seem surreal or nonsensical: the messages may come in a sudden phrase or an impossible image. There's no sequence to what happens. Just observe it.

There are physical and psychological explanations for what your alpha-theta brainwaves are doing when you experience flashes of insight, surreal imagery, or vivid imaginings. It's also possible that spirit guides really are able to connect with you at this mysterious moment between consciousness and unconsciousness.

What hath night to do with sleep? -John Milton

Writing Practice – Slumber with a Key

Hypnopompia occurs as you're waking up—but before you're fully conscious. Become aware of the moment, and try to always write down what you experienced—even if it's only a feeling or an image from a dream you've already forgotten. Take a moment to thoroughly appreciate the transition time between sleeping and waking. The habit enriches your inner creative life—and makes the rest of your day happier.

Hypnogogia, however, is an experience you can create for yourself. Here's how:

At around two in the afternoon, when your energy level is low because of your brain's circadian rhythm, get comfortable in an armchair. Your circadian rhythm is your biological clock that regulates sleep, body temperature, production of hormones, and other things. At around two in the afternoon, your energy is at its lowest, no matter what you've been doing for the rest of the day. Now, decide on a way to stay awake. For example, Thomas Edison held a steel ball in his hand. As soon as he drifted off, the ball fell and woke him up.

Salvador Dali used a key and he calls this exercise "Slumber with a Key" (it's one of his *50 Secrets of Magic Craftsmanship)*. He learned the practice of 'sleep without sleeping' from the Capuchin monks of Toledo. Here are his instructions:

> *"...Seat yourself in a bony armchair, preferably of Spanish style, with your head titled back and resting on the stretched leather back...In this posture, you must hold a heavy key which you keep suspended, delicately pressed between the extremities of the thumb and forefinger of your left hand. Under the key you will previously have placed a plate upside down on the floor. Having made these preparations, you will have merely to let yourself be progressively invaded by a serene afternoon sleep, like the spiritual drop of anisette of your soul rising in the cube of sugar of your body. The moment the key drops from your fingers, you may be sure that the noise of its fall on the upside-down plate will awaken you..."*

Whatever way you decide to stay awake, the purpose of this exercise is to calmly observe your thoughts, rather than to think them. As you drift into hypnagogia, try to stay conscious of what's happening. Perhaps a phrase will come to you, or an image, or you'll feel flooded by emotion. Be relaxed, but also be alert and aware. According to Dali and the Capuchin monks, your revelation will come to you in less than a second.

Keep a journal on hand so you can write down what happens.

If you don't have the opportunity to have a siesta, use the time before you go to sleep at night. It's much harder to get the same results when you're drifting off to sleep at night because 1) you're too tired to concentrate and 2) it's hard to remember what you experienced since you'll usually fall asleep during the exercise. But if nighttime is your only option, try this: Ask yourself a question just before you go to sleep. You might say something like: "I don't know how to end my story. Show me the way. Guide me to the conclusion." You can also ask about something other than writing—something that has made you feel stuck, perhaps.

The next morning, before you wake up, become conscious of your state of being. This is almost like developing a lucid dreaming state, except that you really are awake. Your body doesn't yet realize it is, and so it's unable to move. See if a word, an image, or a feeling merges with you. Sometimes you may experience it just as an intense feeling of joy or grief. Other times there's a sentence that comes at you that may seem random. Pay attention. Notice.

As in all these writing practices, find your own way into this state of being. Whether it's when you're waking up, taking your siesta, or retiring for the night, using hypnopompia will instill within you a combined sense of freedom and guidance.

It is a common experience that a problem difficult at night is resolved in the morning after the committee of sleep has worked on it. -John Steinbeck

Daily Happinesses

kissing the underside of her wrists
a pile of rubies in the sunshine
a statue coming to life and touching your shoulder
fresh pineapple in winter
an admiring glance from a stranger
playing games all night during a blizzard
enveloped in the softest blankets imaginable

WEEK 2

Mirrors should think longer before they reflect. -Jean Cocteau

When you read about a new hat, why do you want one too?

My husband went through a Perry Mason phase a while back. He'd be dozing through the pages, then he'd suddenly jump up and pour himself a glass of scotch. Or he'd glance over at my bare legs on the couch, and I'd know that Della Street had just stepped out of the cab and Perry was eyeing her ankles.

Any avid reader knows the power of a book to transport you into another world, be it a magical realm in a fairytale or a fast-paced thriller.

This is not just because we're wildly imaginative readers. Researchers have found that our brains simulate the events of the book in the same way they process events in the real world. In a study described in the journal Psychological Science some years ago, it was shown that the way our brains process images and written words is linked to the way they process actions we perform ourselves. For example, reading an active verb such as "button up" or "put on your hat" activates the same region of the brain that is activated when we actually do button up or put on our hat.

One thing you can love about writing is that you can make things up. I know that seems obvious, but think about it for a moment. You can make up anything you like! You're free! And, even better, you're making up something that your reader is actually experiencing (sort of).

Take clothing, for example.

Describing clothes is a terrific way to enjoy dressing up without having to. Let your brain simulate the feeling of slipping into a satin black sheath. The shiny fabric gleams in the moonlight, and the pleated bodice might give this deceptively simple gown a unique flair. And are those black diamonds that sparkle as she kicks off her ankle-strap heels and leans back against the sofa, waiting for the doorbell to ring…?

The wonderful thing about dressing your characters is that you can 'wear' all the clothes you either can't afford or you think you wouldn't be able to pull off. Let your imagination run wild and dress your characters with fun and abandon. If you've coveted that wine-and-black silk and lace slip, let your heroine have it for a few hours. Or if that Stetson is something you wish you were brave enough to wear when you visited your mother-in-law, give it to your hero in the interim.

When you have only two pennies left in the world, buy a loaf of bread with one, and a lily with the other. -Chinese Proverb

Writing Practice – Writing about Clothing

Describe a character by only describing their clothing. You can use metaphors and similes, and you can tell a story about the clothing. ("He wore the sumptuous purple cashmere bathrobe that he'd gotten when he was in Milan the summer before—that had been a good time, and wearing the bathrobe reminded him of it." Or: "He wore the sky-blue silk cravat high against his pink, closely-shaved chin, as if he were setting off to his private gentleman's club on Songbird Street.")

Or maybe you imagine a woman walking down the cobblestone street just as the sun is rising, wearing a linen print of coffee, cream, and powder blue, with a sweetheart neckline, and large black buttons up the front. Lace-up espadrilles give her an easy stride. As she nears, you see that her mascara is smudged and her hair's in tangles from her night out on the town—she's had a wonderful time!

Or she's wearing a flowing gown printed in large blocks of lagoon blue, teal, and fog grey—she spreads out the blanket on the beach, takes off her bottle-green sandals, and muses as the sun sets…

Color is one of the juiciest details when you're creating a character through their clothing, but don't just say, "He wore a red vest," and hope that it evokes the character you're describing. Instead say something like, "The red vest he wore made her think of a swashbuckling pirate," or "His suit was somber black, until he reached over to shake her hand, and she was startled by the fire-engine red silk vest he wore underneath. Was he mocking the man who lay in the coffin, just a few feet from them?"

The type of fabric is also good: ruffles, lace, flowing, translucent, smooth, stiff. Avoid words like 'elegant' or 'sophisticated' and instead *show* how the outfit is elegant. "The gown shimmered all the way down her back like a waterfall cascading to the floor." You assume a gown that shimmers and cascades *is* elegant, so you don't have to say so.

Let us be grateful to the mirror for revealing to us
our appearance only. –Samuel Butler

Daily Happinesses

the oldest pine tree in the world
a printed party invitation
Iranian folk music
gold glitter floating upward from her palm
tramping through the snow at dusk
the bray from a neighbor's donkey
creating your own mandala

WEEK 3

Brain, n. An apparatus with which we think that we think.

–Ambrose Bierce

The Art of Meditation

I heard that when the Dalai Lama was asked what he would do if he had fifteen minutes left to live, he replied, "I would meditate."

Why meditate? There are many reasons, and many different types of practices. Some time ago, I heard an interview with a Carmelite nun, in which she was asked about her daily routine. She described the tasks, the meals, the leisure time, and then she said, sounding reverent and happy, "and then it is time for prayer—which is the time we love best." It was said in the same tone that many of us look forward to a party or a date or going out to the theater.

It's how you can feel about your own meditation.

How is meditating a writing practice?

By meditating, you're training your mind to be your servant, rather than you being a servant of your mind. In life, you can get lost in a dizzying array of splendid thoughts and ideas and conversations. Meditation helps to remind you that your head is as useful as your hands for writing, or your feet for walking. But your mind is not your being, your real self. Your mind is useful—but it needs to learn how to be still and empty to make room for creativity and calm.

Additionally, meditating teaches you equanimity, which helps you to feel peaceful even when there are stressful or urgent situations surrounding you. Instead of getting sucked into an emotional, uncontrollable vortex of fear or anger, you remain calm. Emotions are good—when they're kept in balance.

By meditating, you train your thinking to be intentional, not at the mercy of reaction to others' emergencies. When you are tranquil, you help others to be tranquil as well. You also bring that tranquility to your writing practice.

There are all kinds of ways to meditate: you can sit, or whirl. You can walk, but try not to think. Instead, observe what is around you, without judgment. Focus on your breath if your mind starts wandering. Move through the natural beauty that surrounds you, and observe it with compassionate detachment.

Dancing is another form of meditation—sometimes moving to music helps your mind focus, as on a mantra. It's important to be gentle with yourself—I've known some people to get exasperated with their inability to meditate! The mental chatter that tends to overtake us can be overwhelming. But anyone can find a way to find the quiet stillness of one's innermost being. Be patient.

Half the exercise is slowing down, being very still, listening to yourself, listening to the holiness that is you. Peace doesn't come from somewhere outside—nor does happiness or calm. It comes from going inward.

Did you ever stop to think, and forget to start again? -Winnie the Pooh

Writing Practice – Meditate

If you haven't meditated before—or only rarely or with a teacher—here's a beginner's basic:

Find a place where you know you won't be interrupted. Be seated comfortably. Close your eyes. For five or so minutes, focus on your breath. Breathe deeply and slowly. You'll hear your breath going in and out, and you might get twitchy and bored and begin to think of something else. Gently focus your mind back on your breathing.

When images or feelings come to you, imagine they are rafts on a gentle river: just let them pass by. Focus on your slow breathing again.

After five minutes, quietly let go of your concentration and open your eyes.

That's it.

Over the course of the next few weeks, you may want to increase your meditating time to ten or fifteen minutes. Eventually you'll find the time that works best for you. Transcendental Meditation recommends twenty minutes twice a day. Zen monks sit in meditation for six hours a day. Make your meditation practice your own.

If you already know how to meditate, but only do it on occasion, try to do it as a regular practice for a week and observe any changes.

If you're a seasoned meditator, then try a different kind of meditation for a week or two, to stretch and flex your meditation muscles. There are so many varieties to choose from: focusing on a mantra, moving meditation, walking, dancing, whirling, breathing.

It's *your* meditation practice—choose one that works for you.

The world we have created is a product of our thinking; it cannot be changed without changing our thinking. -Albert Einstein

Daily Happinesses

freshly cut wood
receiving a surprise present
a cloak of invisibility
the sweetness of dawn
a tender look
coming home very late from an adventure
having a conversation with a gnome in the garden

WEEK 4

Really, in the end, the only thing that can make you a writer is the person that you are, the intensity of your feeling, the honesty of your vision, the unsentimental acknowledgement of the endless interest of the life around and within you. Virtually nobody can help you deliberately -- many people will help you unintentionally. –Santha Rama Rau

Interviewing: Asking the Question

Whether you're researching for a biography, writing a profile for a magazine article, or even if you're just out on your first date with a new love interest, asking the right questions will give you depth and pleasure in getting to know someone.

This is true especially if you're shy. Being prepared is vital to the experience.

The best interviews are always conversations, and the most important quality you bring to any conversation is your own interest. Your interest is contagious, and makes for a more interesting dialog. Because it is fun to do, it becomes fun to write; because it's fun to write, it is fun to read.

How do you summon interest for a topic or a person? Before a meeting, research as much as you possibly can about the person you're going to meet. If you're researching a story or reporting on an event, get as much detailed information as you can before you begin forming questions. Background details are the bones of an interview, and you don't want to begin an interview without the skeleton.

Your questions are your most powerful tool to creating a conversation, whether for a job interview, a romantic encounter, or researching a biography. So, before you meet, come up with several strong, leading questions. This is how you'll create the energy that makes it interesting. Open-ended questions are the best: these are questions that cannot be answered with a simple yes or no. Ask yourself what is most special about the person? Why have you chosen this individual? Has he/she done anything outstanding? Why do you want to meet and what do you long to know?

"Would you please tell me about yourself?" is the most-often asked question. But how awkward it makes the other person feel! What is one supposed to say to that?

Instead, ask something odd, different, but personal. Be creative.

- "What was the best thing that happened to you this year?"
- "Who is the most important person in your life?"
- "What's your ideal Saturday?"

If you have a specific topic, like you both discover you care about oriental rugs, you could ask:

- "What is the most meaningful rug you've ever owned and why?"
- "Have you ever traveled to the country where it came from? What was that like?"
- "How did you first become interested in oriental rugs?"

Other questions:

- What was the house like where you grew up?
- Where do you hope you'll be in five years?
- Choose five adjectives that describe you.
- Tell me about one thing in your life you're proudest of.
- Describe your ideal teacher/job/home.
- What is your philosophy toward work and play?
- If you won a million dollars, what would you do first?
- If you could live anywhere in the world, where would it be?

Here are some open-ended and follow-up questions:

- What will that mean in the future?
- How did you come to that decision?
- Can you tell me more about that?
- Are you glad you did that?
- Why do you feel that way?

A couple of tips: Avoid long, complex, multi-part questions; usually those answers are confusing or dull. You'll get more intriguing responses to short, straightforward questions. Also, remember not to talk too much, and don't keep re-phrasing a question. That's an easy habit to fall into, especially if you're nervous. Keep the focus on the other person, not on you.

> *I never want to see anyone, and I never want to go anywhere or do anything. I just want to write.* –P. G. Wodehouse

Writing Practice—Know Yourself

Picture yourself after a long journey across a desert. You arrive at the oasis late in the afternoon, and, to your excitement, you learn that someone you've always wanted to meet is staying at the same hotel as you.

That person is *you*.

Shower, nap, relax as you think about what you want to know most of all about yourself. Look at the tips above for help with this. Think about what means more to you than anything else, and focus your interview questions around that.

Now that you're prepared for the encounter, go ahead and meet up. You have your questions ready and your notebook handy, and you know that the interview may well turn into a conversation that you'll cherish as a highlight of your journey.

Get comfortable. Have some tea. Ask your questions, and answer them with as much interest and clarity and depth as you would if you were being asked these questions by the most important person in your life.

Write down the answers.

You might want to take a break before proceeding to the next step, which is to write out the interview as a real profile of a person you love and admire. First, arrange the questions and responses in a logical order. Create an outline. What is the most important thing that stands out for you about this person? Come up with an interesting title for your story about this encounter.

Begin the introductory paragraph with an anecdote. Vivid imagery is a great way to start. Or you could bring the reader into the place where the interview occurred. "As I sat at the café, waiting, I wondered what she would be like. I was worried I might not recognize her. But as soon as she emerged from the hotel on the far side of the plaza, I knew it was her. Her piercing eyes caught mine and...."

In this first paragraph you have to state the person's name (in this case it's you) and why you wanted to meet (this usually melds into the 'something important in your life.'). You can either write the interview in a question-and-answer form, or in a narrative essay form. Either way, you need an introduction, smooth transitions, a logical sequence of thought (you can rearrange the sequence of questions, but you do need to accurately quote your interviewee), and a strong conclusion.

This writing practice is one of the harder ones, but it can be a deeply rewarding experience. We don't self-reflect nearly enough on our own lives, accomplishments, and feelings. Try it.

And remember, no matter where you go, there you are. –Confucius

Daily Happinesses

going to a party in the city
gazing into the eye of a whale
getting on the train and waving goodbye
getting paid for a good job well done
knowing you're safe
singing folk songs with friends late into the night
wind in the sails

February

Week 5 – Don't let your possessions possess you
Week 6 – Love Letters: the most important love letter you'll ever write
Week 7 – Intelligence of the Heart: how to write holistically
Week 8 – In the Garden: a dream of a garden is a key to your spirit

WEEK 5

Men would live exceedingly quiet if these two words, mine and thine, were taken away. –Anaxagoras

Don't Let Your Possessions Possess You

One of my grandmother's—and my mother's—favorite tenets in life was this: "Don't let your possessions possess you."

Traveling as they both did, during tumultuous times, when you could count on very little, and yet both of them owning some of the loveliest items in the world (an antique Renaissance dining table, exquisite Victorian glassware from my grandmother's grandmother, rare Florentine leather-bound books, signed paintings from aspiring and famous artists), it must have been hard to know what was important to keep and what was important to let go.

When my mother was ten years old, she and her family were living in a tiny fishing village in Caldas d'Estrach in Spain. When civil war erupted in the late 1930s, they were rescued by a British destroyer that moved into the bay to evacuate them, since they were the only Americans residing in that area. My mother and her siblings were told they could only bring three items of clothing with them (besides what they were wearing already): a bathing suit, a sweater, and an evening dress.

My father brought his extensive library with him wherever we traveled. What other possessions possessed our family? Silks from India, amethysts from Persia, fragrant herbs… these all seemed of vital importance to my mother. Also, the wooden plates we'd had since the time we lived in Greece and the copper mug my brother made in school… even trying to live as simply as my parents did, some things made the crucial 'to keep' list.

But most possessions were constantly left behind, with neighbors, friends, at a vendor in a flea market in Rome, or at a local charity shop in an English village.

Freedom from too many 'things' made the great adventure of travel, which seemed at the heart of my parents' life together, much more pleasurable.

It is preoccupation with possession, more than anything else, that prevents men from living freely and nobly. –Bertrand Russell

Writing Practice: The last ten things

Imagine this: you are alone on a desert island-like-place, and you can only have ten items for the rest of your life. You have no electricity or form of energy outside what you can create yourself (in other words, no laptop or cell phone). Which ten items would you want to surround yourself with?

Most of the time, these are mine:

- *pencil*
- *paper*
- *guitar (with extra guitar strings)*
- *12 yards of colorful silk (to dance with, clothe myself, keep warm in, use as shelter)*
- *a deck of Tarot cards*
- *a book (the title always changes)*
- *a bed*
- *a pillow*
- *a cup*
- *a pocket knife*

What are yours? Write them down. Then go to the next part of this writing exercise:

Remove five of these most vital possessions in your life. What are you left with?

Now remove two more. Reiterate the situation in your imagination: you're left on a desert island, entirely alone, with only three items for the rest of your life. What are they?

Now remove another.

And another.

So now you discover the one item that you feel you would like to have with you, when all else is gone. For me, the first time I did this, the outcome was a surprise.

I do this exercise for myself every few years or so, and find the first ten items are remarkably stable.

I do it for my main character every time I write a novel, and find it gives me enormous insight into the essence of their being.

As long as our civilization is essentially one of property, of fences, of exclusiveness, it will be mocked by delusions. –Ralph Waldo Emerson

Daily Happinesses

fresh mangoes falling into the hammock
red roofs of Rome
diving into the pool
the greatest kindness
seeing a stained glass window for the first time
brilliant sparkles on the waves
the tallest bridge in the world

WEEK 6

Love has no desire but to fulfill itself. To melt and be like a running brook that sings its melody to the night. To wake at dawn with a winged heart and give thanks for another day of loving. -Kahlil Gibran

Love Letters—the most important love letter you'll ever write

Many great writers were inspired by a real-life muse (like Dante's Beatrice, who didn't have a clue) or even a fantasy (Keats was crazy about a prostitute, who also didn't have a clue). But the fact that they hardly knew each other did not make their love any less poignant, rich, and inspiring.

Elizabeth Barrett and Robert Browning—famously the most romantic couple ever to fall madly in love before they met—used poetry and letters to get to know each other. One wonders what their emotions were like when they first set eyes on each other after having written letters and poems like the ones they did! Was there worry? Curiosity? Disappointment? Or just sheer bliss and joy and an immediate determination to run away together?

Romantic letters are powerful in so many ways. They are a way to be direct and intimate, and they last a long time. Sure, the words that someone has spoken might stay in your memory for a while, and you might re-read them over in your mind, but it's not the same as having them on paper, or saved in your computer's 'letters' folder: something tangible, that you can hold and see. Also, you can write in a letter words that you can't say face to face, things that might feel too embarrassing, or you're anxious about the other person's reaction, or you're too shy.

A letter is a way to get to the heart of your longing. Ultimately, it's not looks, goodness, wealth, nor destiny that makes us fall in love. It's something else entirely—and completely mysterious.

A man is not where he lives, but where he loves. –Latin Proverb

Writing Practice – Write a Love Letter

We're taught in basic marketing and promotion courses that 'you' is the most important word. You simply can't use it often enough. This is because the most important person in your life is *you*. The funny thing about romantic love, and why it can sink us to such despair, is that we think the happiness it supposedly brings us is contingent on someone else. We long for that 'you'—I love *you*...

Here is a different approach: Write a love letter to yourself. Dig deep into the inner recesses of your soul and write out all the wonderful, magical, enticing, and beautiful things about *you*. You can include seemingly small details (like the shape of your eyelid or the inside of your elbow), but always remember that it's not the parts that make a whole person. The whole person is made up of parts.

Have fun with this letter. Feel safe—no one will tease or scorn your effusiveness. Say much, much more than you ever would to someone else. Did you do a good deed that you told no one about? Do you love the way you sing a lullaby to your children? What about your humor, your kindness, even your silliness? This is not a moment for any sort of self-deprecation: imagine how hurt a lover would be if you were at all critical in a love letter! *Ugh*—don't do it! Treat yourself as tenderly and passionately as you would someone you were absolutely crazy about. You can even draw on this letter, decorate it, attach a photograph, a painting, or a piece of music. Sprinkle it with essential oil of rosewood. Share what you love about yourself with you. Most importantly, tell yourself "I love you."

Help me to believe the truth about myself– no matter how beautiful.
–M. Wiederkehr

Once you have completed the love letter to yourself, try writing one to other people in your life. Even if it's someone you've had a rocky relationship with (for example, a friend, or a sibling, or a parent) try this exercise. You don't have to send it to the person—just see how it makes you feel about them.

If you want to gain deeper insight into a character, have them write a love letter to another character. Watch an emotional dimension emerge that perhaps even you, the author, weren't aware of before.

Love is, above all, the gift of oneself. –Jean Anouilh

Daily Happinesses

the island of Delos
being asked for a favor
the sun on your closed eyelids
an old friend from high school
sweeping away the cobwebs
finding a magic charm in the branches
two woodpeckers during a warm spell

WEEK 7

The heart has its reasons that reason knows nothing of. –Blaise Pascal

Intelligence of the Heart

I was always amused by the stories of doctors and philosophers who during the Middle Ages and the Renaissance would cut open a person's corpse to try to locate the soul. Was it in the spleen? Or the gall bladder?

Have things changed much? Not really. It's just that nowadays our current scientific community has pretty much decided that our soul—or 'intelligence'—resides in our brain. It's as though neuroscience is the religion of the times. Recent studies have even proven (supposedly) that the source of love is the brain. By studying rats, these priests of our modern-day society have been able to conclude that there are four tiny areas of the brain that form a circuit of love: the ventral tegmental area, the nucleus accumbens, the ventral pallidum, and raphe nucleus. So, that's that.

Or is it?

The Ancient Egyptians mummified every organ, believing that all of them were extremely valuable in the afterlife. Except for one: They tossed the brain away as useless. Like a simple limb or other tool, it had served its purpose during life, which was a purely physical purpose. And yet we westerners tend to imagine our brains and our minds as being the same as 'us'—our natures, our beings, even our souls.

I pondered this when the holes in my mother's memory got bigger and bigger. Without her 'brain' functioning as a memory device, who was she? She still had the personality, the physicality, the beauty, the generosity, and the warmth of the woman I had known all my life. Where did that 'person' reside? Where did our love for each other reside? It was not in her brain.

So here's another possibility: that our heart has an intelligence and spirit of its own. The idea of intelligence of the heart is described by artists and mystics of every culture who seek the meaning of life. As teachers, they can point the way for us, and be our guides, but our brain-intelligence is unable to know what they teach without our own direct human experience. We can learn facts and figures with our brains, but ultimately our brains are like computers, and we need people and art and experience to bring that knowledge to life, to bring spirit and love and conversation and relationships to all the facts that our brains collects. We need an intelligence of the heart in order to make sense of it all.

This may be why I've always loved reading and writing romantic novels. For me, the connection between people, their emotional intensity, their loss and suffering and overcoming obstacles, their striving, the joy and satisfaction that follow the struggle, the tangled web that weaves a good story, can become as dear to me as real-life relationships.

And for those who enjoy the language of science: even scientists have proved what they refer to as heart intelligence—a sort of independent wisdom inherent to the heart. The support for this idea came when it was discovered (after several mysterious personality changes occurred in recipients of heart transplants) that over half of our heart muscle tissue is embedded with neural cells similar to those found in our brain. Not only that, but our heart is autogenic, meaning it is the only part of our body that does not need our brain or nerves or anything else to make it function; all it needs in order to 'come alive' is the small bit of tissue that's embedded in the wall of our right auricle. There's no external trigger for making it live. The heart may seem to be a hollow muscular organ that operates as a pump to circulate blood, but it's more than that. It has a life of its own.

The mysterious force that brings us to life, and really makes us feel alive, is taken for granted by the brain, which tends to enjoy listening to the endless babble of its own blog-like thoughts. But when our attention is focused on something other than that, like a work of art or an experience in nature, a peace and inner stillness emerges, and we have a different kind of understanding about life, one that has nothing to do with IQ, education, or age. It's heart-understanding, or heart-intelligence.

In this often-told story, Jung relates a conversation he had with a Hopi elder. To the Hopis, Mountain Lake told Jung, white people seem always uneasy and restless: "We do not understand them. We think that they are mad."

Jung asked him why he thought whites were mad.

"They think with their heads," Mountain Lake replied.

"What do the Hopis think with?" Jung asked.

Mountain Lake pointed to his heart.

In the book of life, the answers aren't in the back. –Charlie Brown

Writing Practice – Writing Holistically

What is holistic writing? In essence, it means balancing your strong intellect and your rich emotional life with the actual activity of writing. No writing endeavor can be successful without ensuring that these three qualities are equally drawn on and developed.

Your practice this week is to uncover a story you wrote some time ago. Reread it with a holistic lens. Ask yourself these questions:

- Do I really *know* who my main character is? (intellect)
- Do I *understand* his or her relationship with other people? (emotions)
- In what way does my protagonist *develop* and change? (action)

For each of these three qualities (knowing, understanding, changing) you can go deeper still. Ask yourself this about your main character:

- What does he think?
- What does she feel?
- What does she do?

Ask yourself these same three questions regarding her relationship.

Ask yourself these same three questions regarding the plot and developing story line.

By analyzing a story in this way, you'll find yourself growing more resilient and flexible in your writing.

You'll also find that your writing flows more readily from your heart than your brain. Your brain gets exhausted, depleted. But, paradoxically, the more you use your heart, the stronger and wiser it gets. It nourishes itself the more it nourishes your writing. Its tendency is to overflow.

You can discover more about a person in an hour of play than in a year of conversation. –Plato

Daily Happinesses

a small wave on the pebbles
embers smoldering
taking off your hat
gazing into a selenite crystal ball
waving the magic wand
the Tower card
a wrought-iron gate hidden by holly and hazelnut

WEEK 8

Green fingers are the extension of a verdant heart. –Russell Page

In the Garden: a dream of a garden is the key to your spirit

Why do we love gardens?

Gardens are backdrops to every Arabian Night tale, crucial to Alice in Wonderland's mysterious adventures, vital in several Shakespearean dramas. Whether it is a miniature nature corner in a city apartment or a famous estate designed for an emperor or a queen, the garden is a symbol of something internal and external in each of us. Ideally, of course, the whole world is our garden. But it's also one of the most personal daily aspects of our lives.

Sensual, moving, restful, refreshing, fragrant, our gardens hold qualities of symbolic and spiritual nourishment that make gardening—as a verb—as much as part of our lives as eating, speaking, or loving. All over the world, in every culture, society is comprised of a family, a house, and a garden. In my travels I've encountered hundreds of them: moss gardens and rock gardens in Kyoto, Islamic gardens with waterfalls, intricate tiles, flowering desert plants, and the quiet cypress trees; terraced gardens in Tuscany that brimmed and spilled over with fragrance and color, aromatic herbs, olive trees, potted geraniums and carnations, where we sat at a shady table under an old grape-vine trellis sipping *vino rosso* and savoring *formaggio* and fresh bread. Even in the jungles of India there were gardens: brilliant bougainvillea, hot and sultry hibiscus, and twining vines that gated and ornamented the sacred caves and temples.

In England, the gardens are elevated to the level of genius: the gentle, kind climate inspires blooms and fragrances unmatched anywhere else. Jasmine, wisteria, daffodils; stone paths meandering through carefully planted and lovingly tended shrubs and beds; holly, hazelnut hedges, a swimming lake, gaudy rhododendrons, and exquisite views and shady groves.

In my Hawaiian garden there grew a mango tree, a plumeria tree, and an avocado tree. Enormous orange and blue birds of paradise perched before my eyes as I sat on my lanai. The rich, vibrant colors and the sweet, salty smell of the ocean saturated my senses and permeated my soul. I'll always remember these images: the rustling wet rainforest ... the moon behind coconut fronds... the trade winds blowing white plumeria blossoms across the hammock... the splash of vermilion from the ubiquitous hibiscus... the parade of red ginger and the fragrance of white ginger.

Even when we lived in New York City, we had window boxes from which climbed the bluest morning glories you ever saw. And ivy fell like waterfalls down the side of the brownstone house, brilliant orange impatiens splashed bits of color here and there. Inside our apartment we had miniature gardens for our children: we called these 'nature corners.' Each month we'd change the nature corner to reflect the season, or a seasonal festival, and create a small place of nature and purpose in the corner of our apartment.

My favorite garden of all was the one in Greece, which was actually just a small plot of marble and quartz sparkling in the red earth. Pine trees and olive trees surrounded me, and crows kept me company while I gazed at the mountains in the distance, but the garden itself was untamed, rocky, solitary. The reason I loved it so was that there was very little I had to do except sit on a warm rock and write. That, of course, was my ideal way to garden.

The garden is the poor man's apothecary. –German Proverb

Writing Practice – Secret Garden

They say if you dream of a house, it is a picture of your soul. When you dream of a garden, it is a view of your spirit.

Your practice: sit comfortably and close your eyes. Tell yourself that you want to experience your ideal garden. Then count backward from ten to one, with the intention that when you reach one, you'll find yourself in that garden.

Without opening your eyes, look around. If you see a path in your mind's eye, follow it. Notice the trees. Are there flowers? What colors permeate the overall feel of your garden? Notice things.

There are many gardens, just as there are many parts of oneself. This garden that you're experiencing in your mind's eye is the garden you're going to describe in detail.

When you're ready, count from one to ten, with the intention that when you reach ten you'll be back in your chair, and ready to describe what you saw in writing.

Throughout the week, expand on this garden you've seen. You may even want to do a little research, and use the precise words for the stone you're going to use for the path or the genus of rose that you want to grow. You may want to visit it each day, and see what changes, or other places to explore. If you encounter a bird or beast, greet it, and ask it a question, like, "What do you have to tell me?"

You might want to include a labyrinth or a courtyard. Imagine the landscape, the lake and woods, and the views from various places in your garden. Imagine especially the seasons and the weather.

Don't bind yourself by supposed limitations of wealth, climate, family, or career. Your ideal garden can be imagined as freely as possible. You will find that by describing it in detail you'll discover deep insights into yourself.

You'll discover that writing about nature will be much easier after doing this. You can use this guided walk into your mind's eye when creating a setting for your story. Create the mood of the garden in your story through the precision and detail. You'll find that by visualizing it first, you'll be able to describe it with ease and pleasure.

Give me odorous at sunrise a garden of beautiful flowers
where I can walk undisturbed. –Walt Whitman

Daily Happinesses

hot lentil soup
a long, hot bath on a snowy afternoon
the dancing girl with her zills
clearing skies over Mount Fuji
completing a task
blue lamps on the antique dining table
the wind rising

March

Week 9 — The Soul of Color
Week 10 — Great Dialog (part 1/3)
Week 11 – Great Dialog (part 2/3)
Week 12 — Great Dialog Part 3/3
Week 13 — Simplify

WEEK 9

Colors, like features, follow the changes of the emotions. -Pablo Picasso

The Soul of Color

Originally, the Ancient Greeks named the days of the week after the sun, the moon and the five known planets. The planets were named after the gods Ares, Hermes, Zeus, Aphrodite, and Cronus. The Romans substituted their equivalent gods for the Greek gods: Mars, Mercury, Jupiter,

Venus, and Saturn. Eventually the Teutonic peoples substituted the Latin names for the gods with their own: Tiu, Woden, Thor, Freya. Saturn remained the same.

So from the beginning, the days of the week were connected to various planets, which in turn were connected to a god or goddess. Each of these relates to a color, a metal, a crystal, a personality. Being aware of the color that represents each day can help you weave a pattern of balance and simplicity into your busy life.

How?

For one thing—by keeping it simple. Simplicity is the essence of calm, harmony, serenity. Having to choose between a number of things is stressful. Becoming aware of color can simplify our lives enormously. This is true even in something as basic as deciding what to wear: If it's Friday—a day symbolized by the serene green of Freya-Aphrodite-Venus, the goddess of love—reach for a mint green sweatshirt; no agonizing. If it's Saturday, wear dark blue jeans. At the mind-numbing market, if you can't decide between blueberries or strawberries, let the color of the day be your guide. Accessories are easily decided on as well: reach for those moonstones or pearls on Monday, or the grey and purple silk tie. Not only is this relaxing, but it makes mundane tasks much more fun. When my children were young I'd often avoid arguments by pointing out that they *had* to eat their green broccoli because it was Friday. Or that the red t-shirt was just right since it was Tuesday.

Another way color can help us is by tempering our temperaments. Each color has a different vibration, and each one impacts us differently. Burger King and Dunkin' Donuts have known this for years (all that pink and orange actually *does* make us eat faster). Blue draws us inward to a place a quiet. Yellow *does* lift our spirits. By becoming conscious of all the different colors in our limited spectrum, we balance our natures. Otherwise we might be particularly drawn to reds, and then lose the blue-ness of our interior being. Or we might be fond of green, but forget to absorb the soul of purple. Balancing our melancholic tendencies by wearing yellow, or soothing our anxiety with a peaceful green makes sense.

Here's an abbreviated outline of the soul qualities of each day:

Monday—*Selenes/Luna/Artemis/Diana*: *lavender or dark blue*. The day of the moon is internal, emotional, reflective, a great day for quiet and meditation.

Tuesday—*Ares/Mars/Tiu*: *red*. The warrior god helps us in our search for Self, standing up to others, fighting for the good, working hard...he symbolizes action and energy. In Norse mythology Tiu was the god of war and sky.

Wednesday—*Hermes/Mercury/Woden* is the messenger god. His color is *yellow*. This is a great day to handle communications and accomplish tasks that require mental acuity. Hermes (or Mercury) is known as the god of commerce, communication, invention, and travel. In Norse mythology, Woden is known as the headstrong leader of the wild hunt.

Thursday—*Zeus/Jupiter/Thor*. *Orange*. Kingly. Expansive. Friendly. Opportunity, luck, good fortune. A good day to look at the big picture or start a new project under the generous auspices of Zeus, the Greek king of the gods. Thor is the god of thunder and Roman Jupiter created thunder and lightning.

Friday—*Aphrodite/Venus/Freya. Green.* The goddess of love and beauty appreciates the attention you pay to beautifying your environment and yourself, as well as socializing with those you love.

Saturday—*Cronus/Saturn. Dark blue or black.* Saturn helps with the details: making sure everything is on track in the material world. He's there to help you over the long haul. He's also known as the god of agriculture and time.

Sunday—*Helios/Apollo/Day of the Sun. White.* Apollo is the storyteller, the musician, the poet, the god of light. This is a good day to be creative.

Colors are the smiles of nature. -Leigh Hunt

Writing Practice – Color Conscious

Each day this week make a conscious effort to be aware of the day's color. If it's Thursday: note the orange instances in your life. A coffee cup, a tangerine, a bookmark, a shopping bag … where do you see something orange?

Write down everything you find that is the color of the day and describe the items using the soul quality of that color. Orange is outgoing, it's a balancer between the heart (red) and the head (yellow), it's expansive, it radiates. It's a friendly color. So when you're describing your orange coffee cup, describe it in a friendly, outgoing way. There are so many variations—millions and millions of shades and moods and tones to every color. Burnt orange is not the same as blood orange or pale salmon. Be as specific as you can when you observe the color.

Noticing color enhances your writing because, as with all description, everything you write needs to be relevant. So if your heroine is wearing a blue dress, it needs to express her dreamy, quiet, or *triste* qualities. If the house is painted yellow, it represents cheerfulness. (Unless you want to be interesting and show how the yellow paint is peeling, or how the mustard-dark quality of the yellow depicts the lack of cheer—you can get complicated and unusual here.)

The most important thing is to enjoy becoming more conscious of the gorgeous colors in our world. Heightening our awareness of the days of the week, the gods and goddesses who rule them, and the placement of the planets in the sky, takes us out of ourselves. It's like watching a rose unfurl, or the leaves on the maple tree beginning to turn. Observing the world around us is crucial to balancing all those stories and ideas that happen inside us most of the time.

Color possesses me. I don't have to pursue it. It will possess me always. I know it. That is the meaning of this happy hour: Color and I are one. –Paul Klee

Daily Happinesses

the plop of a hickory nut
new socks
a meaningful dream
meeting a leprechaun
cowbells
holding hands
watching a meteor shower with a friend

WEEK 10

All the information you need can be given in dialog. -Elmore Leonard

Great Dialog—Part 1/3

We talk most of the time—except for when we're not. The gift of language is part of our existence. We communicate with words far more often and easily than we do through writing or even through an expression like a glare or a smile. And yet much of the time, in conversation as in life, things are not what they seem. Words don't necessarily mean what you think they do, or what they mean when you're writing narrative prose. That's because in dialog the words themselves are colored by the people who are using them.

First, a definition: Dialog is characterized by conversation between two or more people. (Think of the word 'two' in various languages: deo, due, dos, deux). A monolog, on the other hand, means 'one'—it's one person's internal thought process ("To be or not to be, that is the question…"). In films, a monolog is often the "voice over."

Great dialog has to sound realistic, but when you read it or hear it, you'll see that it's more subtle than "real" conversations are. Written dialog is not actually how people talk—it's your interpretation of a conversation. It has to be purposeful to your characters' motivation and to the story itself. If you listen carefully to other peoples' conversations, you'll realize that they usually don't respond directly to a question. People have a mysterious inner life that often reacts completely differently to the words that they are using. For example, a young person may be thinking, "What a crazy old fart! What does he know about skateboarding?" If you're writing a scene where the kid is thinking that, you don't have to tell us, but you would show it in his terse, rude response to being admonished by an elderly professor.

If your characters are eating or watching television while they're talking, one of them might be more interested in food or watching television than in the dialog, and the other one might be frustrated by this. But they would not say "I am frustrated." They might say, "Turn that down!" or "Want *more* cake?" (sarcastically). If they are gazing into each other's eyes, their conversation would sound different, more intense.

Avoid writing dialog where a character describes exactly what they're feeling. Very few people ever do that. Even the words "I love you" need to be used sparingly in a romance: conflict, action, description, or humor can convey the emotion more interestingly. That's because most of us try to avoid being hurt or embarrassed, and it's usually hard to drag out from someone else what they're really feeling. When I watch the television show "Friends" I'm always taken aback at how comfortable and safe the characters are with each other. "Are you okay?" "No, I feel awful—he doesn't love me..." Does anyone really say that so bluntly? In "Friends" it works mostly because it's so unlikely that they'd confess to a ridiculous crush or a bad sleepover that it's humorous. Most people use cynicism, lies, humor, and defensiveness to protect their feelings. What would *your* character use? Let them speak for themselves. You might be surprised at what comes out of their mouths. The tone might convey what they're really feeling, while they actually say something completely different.

To write great dialog you need to know your character so well that what they say flows from their mouths absolutely naturally. There can be nothing jarring in a single word they utter. The personality of each character has to shine through in each voice, distinct from one another's.

Pacing is important as well—your characters breathe and respond and feel. Let that come through in the words they use to share their thoughts and emotions. Your voice is like your face: it reveals more about your personality than you have any idea.

We have two ears and one mouth so that we can listen twice as much as we speak. -Epictetus

Writing Practice – Eavesdropping

Eavesdropping is crucial to writing great dialog. I've found that one of the best places to eavesdrop is on a train, where you can be looking out of the window and listening to a conversation going on in the seat behind you without the conversers knowing. Supposedly, J.D. Salinger went to a local coffee shop to listen to the cadence of teens talking to one another—they completely ignored him, which allowed him to really hear the flow of their voices, not just the words themselves.

To get a sense of this flow, you need to let the words drift through you a bit. Don't focus on their meaning, but instead let what the person is 'really' saying come to you, through their tone, their pitch, their quaver. Did you read the novel "Dune" by Frank Hebert? The most fascinating concept in that book is the power of 'voice' to actually make someone do something against their will. Hebert's premise was more interesting than hypnosis because of the complexity involved in training one's voice as a martial art.

Eavesdropping is one of the most underestimated writing tools. Do it all the time, wherever you are. Standing in line, checking grocery shelves, listening to the radio… let go of the idea that you're trying to learn something or find out something from the words, and instead let the music of the voices and the hidden meaning behind the words come to you. Also, listen especially to the two-part music—the "Oh, yeah," and "Really?" and "Mmm."

Without looking at the person who's talking, try to imagine what she's wearing, where he's from, what her religion or political beliefs might be. Especially try to imagine what their shoes look like, just from listening to their voices. (This is a fun game to play with young children, too.)

Eavesdrop—or listen attentively to conversations around you—for a whole week. At parties, at a family dinner, in the classroom, at a restaurant, on the bus, on the subway. Eavesdrop till it becomes a writing habit.

An essential element for good writing is a good ear: One must listen to the sound of one's own prose. -Barbara Tuchman

Daily Happinesses

an unopened letter
a quiet afternoon
the juice of sweet peaches running down your chin
vintage sunglasses
painting in oils
discovering the cove
the sound of the city

WEEK 11

The most important thing in communication is to hear what isn't being said. -Peter F. Drucker

Great Dialog—Part 2/3

Last week you listened, you eavesdropped—you were surprised by nuance, misunderstanding, flow, pitch, tone... Now it's time to write purposeful dialog. By 'purposeful,' I mean dialog that

illuminates characters

moves the story along

and is fun (or harrowing) to read.

How?

Illuminates characters: The dialog you write has to be the *only* dialog your character would say in response to the situation or other person.

Here's an example of five different characters being illuminated:

She says: "I love you."

Depending on his character, he could respond (not just say something) in any of the following ways:

"No way. Really?"

"It's too late."

"I love you too and I've wanted to marry you for the longest time, but I didn't know how to ask you, so will you marry me now? Today? My star, my delight! Oh, how happy I am!"

"*Sure* you do."

He stared at the road ahead, and she couldn't tell what he was thinking. (No dialog needed—we know exactly what he's thinking: 'He's just not that into her.')

You're conveying what the characters are feeling; you're not explaining it. Dialog has to be subtle and requires a light touch. One of the worst things you can do is expatiate on what someone is saying.

Always keep in mind that you're writing a *dialog*—which means that the person who is listening is just as important as the person who is speaking. No one should say something because it's their turn—they need to respond directly to what the other person said.

Moves the story along:

Throughout the dialog, stick like glue to the conflict at hand. If there's no conflict occurring between characters, whether external or internal, there should be no dialog. Remove it.

Dialog is often brief and matter-of-fact, and yet it propels the story forward—sometimes even faster than action or explanation.

How does your character convey information about the storyline? Instead of, "I'm going to have to drive downtown to fix my flat tire now," say: "Damn tire." Don't be pedantic. Instead, imply, infer, argue, tease—show us what's happening through how two or more characters react to each other.

Every event leading up to every line of dialog has to fit together and make sense, as well as being important to the story. Everything that happens afterward has to be relevant to what was said.

Is fun (or harrowing) to read:

Good dialog does not sound like actual speech. It's rare that including the 'you know' and 'err' will make your dialog more successful. The best dialog needs to sound natural, not 'real.'

Conversation is not linear, like a plot tends to be. Interruptions, misunderstandings, description, and action are all part of dialog, and create tension, emotion, and build relationships.

Don't use dialog to explain something about the story: Always be writing from the heart and mind of the character. It helps to place the characters in an environment that readers can visualize. That crazy thunderstorm during King Lear's descent into madness highlights the dialog wonderfully.

Describe the surroundings and characters' mannerisms as they talk. This makes for a richer read. Intersperse your dialog with description: tell us where they were walking, how they looked, the lines on a forehead, the yellow asters on the black table…

Avoid what are known as 'tags': "he barked" or "she expostulated." Just use "said." Your dialog should convey the bark or the expostulation.

This is controversial, but you probably should avoid phonetic spelling unless there's a real purpose to it. Writing in dialect can be distracting, and less is usually more. (There are brilliant exceptions to this, as in everything.)

Remember that people breathe while they speak—the breaks and rhythm, the cadence, the personality, the music are all important when you write dialog.

The most precious gift we can offer anyone
is our attention. –Thich Nhat Hanh

Writing Practice – How to Write Dialog

There are two parts to this writing practice

This is the scenario: *Joe is getting ready for a job interview. He showers, dresses in his best suit, debates over the right tie, prints out a clean copy of his resume, and packs it into his otherwise empty briefcase. He checks the mail: Uh oh. More past-due notices. No time to open them now. He's going to be late if he doesn't hurry. He starts walking and takes a short cut through a busy farmer's market. A small boy bumps into his leg, sobbing that he can't find his mom. Joe is a warm-hearted man, and wants to help Bobby look for her, but he's already late for his interview. And all those unpaid bills are pretty scary.*

First part:

Close your eyes. Picture Joe. Hear Joe's fast stride as he tries to push through the crowds. Picture the farmer's market. Picture Bobby. Imagine Joe's consternation at being faced with a forlorn young boy who's lost. What on earth is he going to do?

Take your time with this—at least five or ten minutes. Breathe into the scene. Then open your eyes and write down what Bobby and Joe say to each other. Take up a couple of pages and move the story along through the dialog.

In this draft, don't use any words outside of the dialog quotes. Don't even say "Bobby said" or "Joe said." We should be able to know who is speaking just from the sound of their voices. One is a young child; the other is a middle-aged man.

Write as fluidly as you can. Don't edit, don't correct grammar, don't criticize how they talk. Try to let it happen on its own. See how they respond to each other when given their freedom. If you really let them do this, you'll see how they have two very distinct voices, how they really care about their own problems but are conflicted by the encounter, how they engage, change attitude, and how the conversation develops into a relationship.

Remember to stick to the conflict between the two characters. As we said earlier, if there is no conflict between the two characters during a piece of dialog, then the dialog has no place in your story. In this case the conflict is internal (Joe is late for a critical appointment but feels compelled to help Bobby).

Second Part: Read what you've read. Now fill it in: add setting, speech tags, thoughts, and anything else that will flesh out the encounter you just described through dialog. You need to convey Joe's distress and anxiety because of the job interview and Bobby's distress over not being able to find his mom, but without dwelling on either of those things. Have them get to know each other—Joe could get him an ice cream, they might sit on a bench, they might seek out a police officer. Have them discover things about each other on a much deeper level than just money worries and being lost.

What's interesting about writing dialog this way is that the flow of conversation is much more natural than it is if you set the scene first and then add the dialog afterward.

Hopefully, your dialog has evolved into your writing a creative and satisfying conclusion to this story as well.

Courage is what it takes to stand up and speak; courage is also what it takes to sit down and listen. –Winston Churchill

Daily Happinesses

dreams filled with vivid, rich colors
the desert in the evening
boarding the yacht for dinner
faithfulness
dried leaves falling slowly in a still afternoon
getting organized
heroes

WEEK 12

Let us make a special effort to stop communicating with each other, so we can have some conversation. -Mark Twain

Great Dialog—Part 2/3

Just as in life itself, there are three key components to every story, no matter how short or long, simple or complex: People. Space. Time. In other words, characters, situations, events. For a story to work well, all three of these have to connect with each other in a relevant way. If you include an event that has nothing to do with the story, it is obviously disposable. The same with dialog: Wherever you include dialog, it has to be relevant to the unfolding of the story. If it's not relevant, cut it out.

So this is the third part of the Writing Great Dialog triad: you'll need to pare down your dialog to its bone. You're going to edit out every extraneous phrase, cough, word, even comma. If it's not relevant to showing us what your characters want (motive) and how their relationship conflicts with that motive, it shouldn't be in there. There's no room in a good story for pointless chitchat. Your dialog needs to drive your story along, reveal the heart of your characters, show us something surprising or crucial.

If you're not sure whether something is relevant, ask yourself why your characters are talking with each other, and provide an answer. Then see if the phrase is relevant.

Some tips:

Don't forget that we rarely say a person's name when we're speaking to them. Make clear who's speaking by using tags or with some sort of action—don't cheat by saying, "Well, Alonso, so how are you today?" Also, when you use a question mark in the dialog, do you really need to add 'he asked'? Very rarely, if ever. Let your dialog speak for itself.

It may seem picky, but punctuation matters in writing dialog. Use periods correctly, and remember that periods, commas, question and exclamation marks all go inside the final close-quotation mark. (In the U.S., anyway.)

Here are a couple of other punctuation tips: If someone is interrupted, use an em dash. You can use em dashes to interrupt yourself as well—like this, as a side thought—but then go back to the main point you're trying to make. Don't overdo it! Use ellipsis if the thought isn't complete ... or you're implying vagueness ... or some other drifty mood ...

If other people are going to talk, conversation becomes impossible. -James Whistler

Writing Practice: Polishing your dialog till it shines.

1. Edit

Read each word, each phrase, and ask "Is this word vital?" If it isn't, scratch it out.

Don't try to rewrite a phrase; be brave about slicing it out and tossing it aside. Most speech is half as long (at least) as it's usually written.

2. Read Your Dialog Out Loud

Find a closet or take a walk in the woods where no one can hear you except for wild animals. Then read your dialog out loud as loudly as you possibly can (not shouting, though). Listen carefully, and try to stay neutral and detached. How does it sound, heard that loudly? This is an excellent way to test your work. If you can bear to hear it resounding through a canyon, then it will probably stand up to other people reading it.

3. Listen to Someone Else Read It Out Loud

Finally, ask a friend to sit at your kitchen table and read your dialog out loud. (This time at a normal pitch.) You can give them a brief introduction to the two characters, particularly mood and age. Tell your friend, "Alonso is an old man who's lost a valuable piece of jade; he's pretty upset about it. Sally, his maid, stole it, but is pretending to be concerned and helpful." That way your friend will know that one character should sound petulant and cross and the other caring but defensive. You'll be able to hear if your words match the tone the dialog is supposed convey.

Listen carefully, not so much for the words, but for the quality of the back and forth. If a word jumps out at you as being slightly awkward, it probably needs to be tossed or changed.

Dialog is a place in writing where the words should become almost invisible and only their implication is revealed.

Silence is one of the great arts of conversation. –Marcus Tullius Cicero

Daily Happinesses

a feeling of belonging
fresh squeezed orange juice
kindness and generosity
drawing the velvet drapes and turning around
sailing into a harbor for the first time
sharing some good memories
a hug before dinner

WEEK 13

How many things are there which I do not want. –Socrates

Simplify

Simplifying is one of the finest things in life—right up there with making love, doing nothing, and walking in the woods. The empty plot of earth that doesn't have anything planted yet is one of the most magical things in the world. So is the moment before the music starts. Or the sweetness of a haiku. An empty shelf. The beach at dawn. Your child's face. A blank notebook.

In the I-Ching, the hexagram called Wei-Chi means Before Completion. It's the hexagram of extraordinary optimism—opening the way to the future. Everything is on the verge of great abundance, but the transition from chaos to order is not yet completed. The change is prepared for, but there is still responsibility—it's time to set things in order. It's the stillness before the celebration. The anticipation before the great meeting. With this hopeful outlook, the I-Ching "Book of Changes" comes to a close, exemplifying that with every end comes a beginning.

It's springtime.

This is a great time to eliminate things you don't need any more. Old sweaters, a pile of books you keep for sentimental reasons, a routine that's become a bore, a knickknack, old letters, old habits, prejudices, thoughts. Throw them away—or give them away if they're worthwhile—and leave room for something new to come your way. Empty your closets of things you haven't used in a year and allow space in your life. Don't fill the drawer—leave it empty. Clear a shelf—and don't put anything on it. Clear an hour—and don't make plans. Choose not to buy, or plant, or prettify. Don't purchase that new hat. If you clear away old leaves and leave a plot of earth, you might be amazed what emerges. If you clear your life of things that are no longer vital, you'll feel a thrill equal or more intense to the one you'd feel if you'd bought a new dining set.

Be clear about what matters. Simplify your life, your home, your routine, your relationships. Keep the vital ones, empty the rest. Be clear, be empty. And watch what happens.

Simplicity is the ultimate sophistication. -Leonardo DaVinci

Writing Practice – "Good Prose is Like a Window Pane"

When in doubt, throw it out. As you look at individual words in your story or essay, ask yourself whether or not it's vital for them to be there. You might be surprised how much more powerful and convincing your writing can become by eliminating clutter. By paring your piece to its essence, you are allowing the words to speak for themselves. They don't need you, the author, to give them a crutch or that extra drink.

Here's an example:

"She moaned again, burying her face in her hands. We waited for something – no one knew what – to happen next. Harry was taking a long time getting the glass of water."

Do you see which word is purposeless and annoying? Yes, you got it! "Next." What the heck is it doing there? Completely unnecessary! See what I mean?

Here's something George Orwell said: "One can write nothing readable unless one constantly struggles to efface one's own personality. Good prose is like a window pane."

You don't want words to get in the way of your writing—you want them to *be* the writing.

I'm reminded of my yoga teacher's instruction: to let your breathing breathe itself.

Let your writing write itself.

Daily Happinesses

French onion soup on a cold day
a storm over Tintagel
Varanasi, on the banks of the Ganges River
laughing in the kitchen while you wash dishes together
changing the furniture around
a child asleep in your arms
an affectionate cat

WINSLOW ELIOT
WriteSpa
Writing through the year . . .

April

WEEK 14

No matter how long the winter, spring is sure to follow. –Proverb

Spring Gets in Your Eyes

One spring when I was sixteen, my friend Carol visited me where I lived in Sussex, England. We took many long walks through Ashdown Forest or into the village of Forest Row. Both of us being philosophical in nature, we spent a lot of our time talking about the purpose of life and other fun things like that. Since it was springtime, we talked about why April was considered "the cruelest month," and why more suicides occur in spring than at any other time of the year, and how it was that beauty and sadness seem almost synonymous in Keats' Ode on Melancholy. ("But when the melancholy fit shall fall/Sudden from heaven like a weeping cloud/That fosters the droop-headed flowers all/And hides the green hills in an April shroud/Then –") We also noticed that the most startling quality of spring, especially in areas of severe winter, is the surprising color that constantly amazes. Just a single purple crocus or a few waving daffodils can take your breath away.

One of Carol's and my favorite activities those few weeks we were together was to take long walks with our eyes closed. Sometimes we held hands, but mostly our hands were vaguely out in front of us so we wouldn't bump into hazelnut hedges or a silver birch… We walked with delicate care, feeling every root and pebble under our sneakers, smelling the most interesting, unidentifiable fragrances, hearing an approaching person from a long way off, talking very little.

Sounds, especially, were heightened. We soon were able to distinguish bird calls we'd never noticed before. The whisper of each breeze was magnified. We felt soft misty rain intensifying on our noses and foreheads and outstretched fingertips in a completely new way. Smells became more vivid. To our surprise, our sensitivity to smells in particular lasted well after our long walks were over. It was as though we'd polished a dulled part of ourselves into heightened consciousness, simply by closing our eyes for a while.

Only once during all those walks did my eyes unintentionally flutter open. The sound of a brook was getting louder, and I worried we might fall in. I glanced at Carol, who was quietly and steadily maneuvering a muddy path along the side of the brook, with her eyes fastened closed. She was heading toward the wooden bridge that we both knew was there. She felt for my hand, and I hastily closed my eyes again, and I didn't open them again till, an hour later, we had arrived back home.

Perhaps the truth depends on a walk around the lake. –Wallace Stevens

Writing Practice – Walking

If you can, take a walk with your eyes closed. If that's not possible, then use your imagination.

Write about your sightless walk. Imagine the experience from the point of view of someone who has no idea what the sounds, and feelings, and smells represent. How do you describe the fragrance of violets if you don't know what a violet is and, especially, what a shy cluster of violets by the side of the stream looks like? How do you describe the sun-warmed bark of an oak, if you don't know what a tree is?

How can you do this? It's hard. Imagine being in the Garden of Eden and naming things for the first time. Are you naming a violet because of its extraordinary color, or because of its elusive fragrance, or its purpose (does a violet have a purpose—like, say, a typewriter?). How do you describe anything without describing its function in our lives—whether that function is pleasure or usefulness? If I'm asked to describe Carol (two legs, two arms, hair, nose, etc…), I'm not describing Carol. Even if I describe her function in life—whether she's a student, a teacher, a successful CEO—that's still not the essence of "Carolness." How do you describe that?

As you practice this way of writing, you'll find something interesting happens. You become increasingly aware of everything around you. Everything becomes imbued with some sort of story. You become the artist, who paints a red door, for example, and instead of just seeing a red door, you see a young lover anticipating her first kiss in the garden just beyond... or the dawn after a harrowing deathbed scene…

Take Van Gogh's painting of a pair of shoes, for example. He creates a story in the painting: he shows us more than just shoes. Through mere brushstrokes, he describes their owner (Heidegger imagines she's a peasant woman with a "toilsome tread"). The purpose of the shoes and the spirit of the wearer are inextricable. "In the stiffly rugged heaviness of the shoes," Heidegger writes, "there is the accumulated tenacity of her slow trudge through the far-spreading and ever-uniform furrows of the field swept by a raw wind. On the leather lie the dampness and richness of the soil. Under the soles slides the loneliness of the field-path as evening falls."

When you're writing, you are transcending the usefulness and obviousness of daily objects, feelings, experiences. You are setting them free to become themselves. You're creating a world—and helping your readers to see things as they really are, through your artist's eye.

The night walked down the sky with the moon in her hand.
–Frederick L. Knowles

Daily Happinesses

a sense of honor
packing donations for a good cause
not spending money
forget-me-nots
singing your heart out
moonlight in Vermont
an emerald pendant sparkling in the morning sun

WEEK 15

"*Words have weight, sound and appearance; it is only by considering these that you can write a sentence that is good to look at and good to listen to.* –Somerset Maugham

Assonance

What a lovely word!

All writers have a natural instinct for using and appreciating assonance. It means to create a resemblance of sound in a phrase by repeating the same or similar vowel sounds.

Sometimes I imagine that language was birthed through assonance—that exquisite, subtle combination of sound and meaning. The dawn of language must have been punctuated by a grunt of love or whisper of fear or murmur of contentment.

The history of language—one of my most cherished subjects—can be very briefly illustrated as a development of meaning into symbol:

Dawn of language: Assonance—only sound carried the meaning of what we said.

Morning: Words were formed to symbolize the meaning of the grunt or murmur.

Noon: Writing was invented in picture-form: illustrations or pictograms to symbolize the words.

Mid-afternoon: The early alphabets were created, which became symbols for the pictograms.

Evening: to be discovered.

Night: ?

Symbols are tremendously important in our lives, because although a thing can be destroyed, the symbol of it cannot. We use symbols far more than any of us realize. Every word we write is really just a symbol for its meaning. In the pictograms of Ancient China, the word mountain was three upside-down 'vees' side by side: a drawing of a mountain!

Or take the word 'quarrel',' which was depicted as three women under a roof. These pictures evolved into symbols that by now you'd have trouble connecting to the original picture, even in Chinese. Later the Phoenicians began to form the earliest alphabets to symbolize parts of the word. What that did, eventually, was to separate a universal language of grunt and feeling (like math or the universally understood STOP sign) into hundreds of different languages with hundreds of different sounds and meaning.

The wonderful thing about the development of language is that we humans have a medium that can convey the spectacular richness of our existence. Throughout the evolution of human consciousness, language has evolved more than anything else in human beings. It's moved from grunt to some of the most awe-inspiring, beautiful, complex stories and poems that can be dreamed.

Love language. It's an extraordinary gift that has been developed wisely for thousands of years.

Take care of the sense, and the sounds will
take care of themselves." -Lewis Carroll

Writing Practice – Assonance

As a writer, you may be hardly aware of the rhythm and sounds that emerge in your writing—but for any good writer it's instinctual. In this writing practice, make it conscious. Practice writing assonantally.

The word stems from Latin 'assonare': 'ad' means to respond to and 'sonare' means to sound. When you write assonantally, you're inspiring your readers to respond emotionally to the quality of the sound in your words.

Usually we're trying just to express ourselves as clearly and succinctly as possible. In this practice, be more subtle. By writing assonantally, you're not only relying on the meaning of the word to set the tone. Assonance affects your reader more like a painting or a piece of music does.

Her feet were smeared in the green sea. The sky cleared briefly – then rain began to fall again. She waited, feeling strange, in the gray dawn for the rest of the party.

The repetition of similar vowel sounds in an assonant poem or paragraph gives you extra power over your reader. Oohs and aaahs, for example, create a sense of awe. Ohs and ayes may create a sense of longing. Play with your moods – read your prose piece or poem out loud. It's the only way you'll hear whether it's working.

(By the way: Assonance also means that you're in agreement, generally speaking. For example, if someone tells you that gardening is the most perfect activity for a summer afternoon, you might be in assonance – but you also respond by saying that lying in your hammock is just as pleasurable. If you disagree, you'd experience dissonance.)

Everybody should have his personal sounds to listen for – sounds that will make him exhilarated and alive or quiet and calm. -Andre Kostelanetz

4-25-14

Daily Happinesses

the upper lip of a newborn baby
a Byzantine icon
sailing to the Outer Hebrides
in the still of the night
opening to the first page
a flurry of love letters exchanged
lighthouses

WEEK 16

We sometimes encounter people, even perfect strangers, who begin to interest us at first sight, somehow suddenly, all at once, before a word has been spoken." –Fyodor Dostoevsky

Never Be Inhospitable to Strangers

Shakespeare & Co, a bookstore on the Rive Gauche in Paris, is a place that changed my life. At seventeen, I had arrived for a month of studying at the Alliance Française. Because of a mix-up with a friend, something that I did not tell my parents about before I left England, I arrived in Paris with no place to stay and hardly any money (this was in spring of 1974—way before credit cards or ATMs—and I literally brought only a few pounds with me. Enough for the course at the Alliance, miscellanies like food, and travel back to London.)

In my dreamy haze of confusion about what to do while in Paris in the springtime, I did the only thing natural to me: I found myself in a bookstore. I still don't know how I got there. Even at the time I didn't really know where I was; I just remember vaguely knowing that eventually night would fall and before that happened I better have a place to stay.

Instead, I spent hours and hours wandering up and down the three flights of grimy stairs, reading, pausing, amazed at everything I found there. I became lost in a world so wonderful I wanted to weep. For those of you who don't know, Shakespeare & Co was home to authors and writers and travelers for years and years. There were letters pinned to the walls from E. Hemingway, Gertrude Stein, Scott Fitzgerald, James Joyce, and many others, personally addressed to the former owner, Sylvia Beach.

When I was there Sylvia Beach was long gone, and instead there was a wise-looking man seated at the desk by the front door. As I wandered the store, and rested on the various couches and deep musty armchairs, reading and exploring, I knew all the time he was aware of me. As dusk started to fall, I made my way toward him and asked if he knew of an inexpensive place where I could stay the night. I expected he'd direct me to a youth hostel or a cheap pension. Instead he looked at me with the most piercing eyes you've ever seen and demanded, "Are you a writer?" I remember answering with complete honesty (although with faint shame that I was as yet unpublished): "Yes, I am." And he replied, "Then if you're a writer, you can stay here." He didn't ask where I'd been published, or what kind of things I wrote, or anything like that. He took it for granted that I was a writer, because I said so.

It was as though he had seen my soul.

Looking back, I think George Whitman (yes, it was him!) saw my soul more clearly than I did. He was the angel welcoming me into a tribe. For three days I stayed at this magical bookstore. It was open all through the night, hosting writing workshops, groups, meetings, friends. Writers met, drank coffee, talked, slept, drank more coffee, talked, wrote, and read. During a workshop someone would lie down on a couch and doze for an hour, then get up and join back in. Late in the morning sometimes the doors closed so we could close our eyes briefly, but most of the time the place was alive with Writers and Writing. I remember washing out cups of coffee in the makeshift kitchen and realizing with a profound shock: "This is it. I am a *writer.*" I was no longer a stranger.

Years later I learned much more about George Whitman, and the extraordinary impact he's had on so many people and on the cultural life of Paris and literature.

One of his most famous quotes, that I continue to live by, is: *"Never be inhospitable to strangers, lest they be angels in disguise."*

Writing Practice – The Stranger

The idea of a stranger conjures up all sorts images. On the one hand, it's romantic. Tony Bennett sings, "I'm a stranger in paradise ...." Frank Sinatra sings: "Strangers in the night..." Danielle Steel writes about that "Perfect Stranger."

On another hand it's sinister. Patricia Highsmith novel "Strangers on a Train" has one of the deadliest concepts of what being strangers really could mean. (They each commit the other's desired murder, so nothing can link them to the crime. Hitchock's film is based on Highsmith's novel.)

Strangers can be messengers in a fairytale, someone wise to give advice, or an angel. Strangers can also kidnap, be cruel, or be a wanderer, never at home anywhere in the world. People who stay at home talk about strangers, and generally distrust them.

A stranger in a story sometimes has a mystical or religious purpose. Clarence in *It's a Wonderful Life* is a stranger.

Albert Camus wrote about self-alienation in *L'Etranger*. In the twentieth century, humans became strangers even to themselves.

What does it mean to be a stranger?

What's *your* story about a stranger?

In the short story you're going to write this week, imagine a life-changing experience for which the catalyst is a stranger. Center your theme around this quote: "Never be inhospitable to strangers, lest they be angels in disguise."

You don't have to include the phrase in your story, but make it a central aspect.

Encounter a stranger and see what happens. Don't plot this out before you begin. Start writing and let the stranger show up in his or her own way. Let the story tell itself. You might be surprised by what happens.

Sometimes you have to get to know someone really well to realize you're really strangers. –Mary Tyler Moore

Daily Happinesses

the bonfire dying down
jumping higher than ever before
the seat of your pants sticky and bright
from sliding down the rainbow
on the back of a giant sea turtle
candles at twilight
raising a barn
courage

WEEK 17

Any man who can drive safely while kissing a pretty girl is simply not giving the kiss the attention it deserves. –Albert Einstein

Kisses

How do we write about kissing and kisses and all the delightful pleasurable possibilities that accompany one of the loveliest activities in the world?

Now, I'm not necessarily just talking about kissing on the mouth, or having fun with tongue. What about those extraordinary moments when a stranger kisses your arm with a fingertip? Or the spring sunshine kisses your eyelids? Or a lover you thought you knew well surprises you with kisses on the back of your knees or the underside of your wrist?

The thing to remember when you write about kisses—and, even better, when you experience them—is to become aware of all your five senses. Don't get lost in your head. That's why surprise is so marvelous: it brings you instantly into the moment. So stop thinking about where this relationship is going (or where it's been), and instead become conscious of the temperature of the air around you, the fragrance of the pikake lei, the salty waves buoying you. Listen to the owl hoot or the music from a neighbor's piano floating through an open window. Taste and touch are good, but so are smell and sound. By becoming aware of sensation, you become aware of being in the present moment, and when you're in the present moment with a kiss, it's magnified a thousandfold.

You don't have to be in a relationship to experience kisses. Kisses come in every form: in the breeze, or meeting your lips in a mirror, or kissing a rose, or snuggling with your cat. Think about kisses as a blessing, and remember that you can bless yourself—you don't need someone else to do it for you.

It takes a lot of experience for a girl to kiss like a beginner.
–Ladies Home Journal, 1948

Writing Practice – Writing about Kisses

Practice the art of surprise. If you don't have a lover to practice this with, use nature or a pet. Be creative. See that tree, with the sap running through its veins with the passion of springtime? What does it feel like to press your lips against its gorgeous bark?

Every day for one whole week, find something different to kiss and then write a detailed description of the experience. See that door that you go through every day? Maybe you haven't really paid attention to it—seen its lovely wood, or the scratch that reminds you of a story. Doors are portals into yourself: kiss the door and write down what it feels like (remember to use all your senses—what do you hear? Is there a dog barking somewhere? Is it windy?)

Be creative in your kisses. Kissing your child's forehead when she doesn't expect it brings joy to you both. Kissing your puppy brings you joy—that's why people cuddle and kiss puppies! Kissing is a good thing.

But you don't need a child or a puppy to experience that joy—kiss your life. Surprise yourself.

Kissing is like drinking salted water. You drink, and your thirst increases. –Chinese Proverb

Daily Happinesses

snuggling into the sleeping bag
fresh beignets for breakfast
a friendly arm around your shoulder
real gold coins pouring down your chimney
redemption
lace gloves and silk stockings
making sense of things

May

Week 18 – Elemental Beings
Week 19 – Nonsense Makes Us Smarter
Week 20 – What is Your Internal Age?
Week 21 – The Nose Knows

WEEK 18

A lady, with whom I was riding in the forest, said to me, that the woods always seemed to her to wait, as if the genii who inhabit them suspended their deeds until the wayfarer has passed onward: a thought which poetry has celebrated in the dance of the fairies, which breaks off on the approach of human feet. –Ralph Waldo Emerson

Elemental Beings

When I was around seven years old, I visited my grandmother, Ethel Cook Eliot, at her home in western Massachusetts. One night she sat on the edge of my bed and told me about some rain goblins she'd seen. She described them to me: eight inches tall, skinny, wrinkled, brown-skinned, leaping in spirit. Her description was so detailed and vivid that I knew without a doubt she actually had seen these creatures.

My grandmother saw other elemental creatures as well, and wrote about them in her extraordinary children's books: *The House Above the Trees, The Wind Boy, The Little House in the Fairy Wood,* and others. One of the most interesting qualities I find in her books is her ability to describe our world from the point of view of an elemental being. Here's an example from *The House Above the Trees,* when lonely Hepatica is being teased, turns away, and encounters a gorgeous Wind Creature.

"Now Hepatica had sometimes, though rarely, seen Wind Creatures before, but always from the factory window and then only in the rush of their passing. Never had she seen one so close.

This Wind Creature looked to be about twelve or fourteen years old. He was walking along the edge of the road, his purple wings folded down his back. He was dressed in a purple tunic just to his knees, a garment not unlike the sky-blue slip Hepatica was wearing, except that his was the color of early morning. His head was tilted back as he walked, his joyous eyes scanning the treetops. He noticed the children, however, as he drew near, and lowered his gaze to them.

They were all up on the stone wall now, jeering at Hepatica. She stood down by the dusty road, her back to them, her eyes clear as the day.

The Wind Creature noticed the children, but only as you might notice flowers, in the same impersonal way. He looked at them directly in their faces without expectation, for he knew very well that they could not see him, that he was not so much as a shadow to them. For never had this Wind Creature known a human child who could see the Forest People.

So his glance passed over the daintily-frocked little girls with their butterfly bows and the boys with their cropped curls, and was just about to pass over clear-eyed Hepatica, when it stopped short; for, wonder upon wonders, she was looking directly at him and smiling in a friendly fashion.

He could hardly believe his eyes. But he smiled back. No one could have helped it, so welcoming and expectant was Hepatica's face. But in his amazement he did not speak to her. Instead, he backed out of the road, and still looking and smiling at Hepatica, moved backward into the green forest that came down to the other side of the road. The evening sunlight struck level through the trees and almost at once Hepatica lost him in the golden glare it made."

Imagine if you looked at a flower and it smiled directly back at you!

No child but must remember laying his head in the grass, staring into the infinitesimal forest and seeing it grow populous with fairy armies. -Robert Louis Stevenson

Writing Practice – Short Story

Write a short story from the point of view of an elemental being.

No matter what you believe, for this exercise bring an elemental being to life. Imagine—even if you don't think it's true—that flowers have fairies living on them and each tree has a tree spirit within it. Imagine that elementals surround us, even if you aren't able to see or hear them because you are limited by the five senses of your physical body.

Choose an elemental that intrigues you. Each elemental being is connected to a particular element—thus the name. Fairies, elves, gnomes, dryads or wood nymphs, and crystal beings are connected with earth. Sprites, mermaids and mermen, and undines are associated with water (my grandmother also wrote about the blue water babies who traveled bubbling streams all over the world). Sylphs and imps are air beings. Salamanders are associated with fire. We think of dragons as a fire elemental, but they are linked to all the elements. All these creatures work and play together to keep our mother earth in harmony and balance.

You can imagine each creature's nature by delving into the nature of its element. Try to get into the spirit of this being. A dryad, or tree nymph, will have a tree-like spirit, rooted in the ground and swaying in a breeze. Water creatures tend towards travel and adventure. Fire spirits move quickly and exude sparkle and light—what kind of picture would they have of our world? What are earth creatures, like elves and goblins, really like?

Here are some prompts for your story:

Elementals love communication with humans—so bring conversation into your story.

They tend to mirror back to us how we are—so if you're kind and generous, they will be as well.

Ask how you can help them (if you don't see or hear them, watch for other ways that they're letting you know what they'd like from you). You can also ask a favor from them. In return leave a gift to show your gratitude. Anything sparkly, sweet, or lovely is welcome.

Elemental beings care deeply about our environment, all animals, plants and flowers, as well as humans.

Sing and dance—they love playfulness, fun, and laughter.

Have this creature encounter a human, and write the story around that encounter. Bring in all the wisdom you can imagine such an elemental creature has garnered through millennia. Give them personality, characteristics, motive. Give them feeling. A heart is not just a place where blood is pumped—a heart is where the spirit resides. Give your elemental being a real heart that only a human can truly understand.

The iron tongue of midnight hath told twelve;
lovers to bed; 'tis almost fairy time. -William Shakespeare

Daily Happinesses

going for a walk before dawn
sitting on a chair and watching ants go in and out of their hole
the musk rose full of dewy wine
walking through falling blossoms
shadow puppets and fireflies
weeding for an hour at twilight until it's too dark to see

WEEK 19

I like nonsense, it wakes up the brain cells. Fantasy is a necessary ingredient in living, it's a way of looking at life through the wrong end of a telescope. Which is what I do, and that enables you to laugh at life's realities. –Dr. Seuss

Nonsense Makes Us Smarter

A paper published in Psychological Science proposes that being disoriented makes the brain work harder and better. The two authors, Travis Proulx and Steven J. Heine, claim that our brains have evolved in a way that we are able to make predictions, and one way we do that is by identifying patterns. We don't like feeling uncomfortable; we don't like what we don't know.

The research expounds on what travel writers have always known: a feeling of disorientation inspires creative thinking. If something doesn't make much sense, we do our best to make it make sense. Andy Warhol was a master at disorienting us, as were the Surrealists: Salvador Dalí in particular. When we look at their art, we're startled, and afterwards we see the world around us slightly differently. Apparently, this is a function of our brain as much as our art-loving heart: our brain is always eager to make sense of everything around us.

Heidegger explains this better than just about anyone I've read: a hammer is not a hammer when you describe what it looks like or how it feels; it is not a hammer without its purpose being described as well. Additionally, a hammer cannot have a purpose without someone there to put it to use. In other words, a hammer cannot exist in and of itself.

Its purpose has to make sense to us in order for it to exist as the object we mean when we say "hammer."

Without explaining the purpose of something, without making sense of it, it becomes nonsense.

For many of us, this is a 'duh' kind of thinking, I suppose. Every day we're supposed to try to see the world as new. Juxtaposing something unusual into your daily routine freshens your mood, makes you alert and interested. That's what happens when you travel or meet someone new. As teachers, we know that the best way to engage a student is to challenge them to think about something in a different way.

As part of their research, Dr. Proulx and Dr. Heine asked twenty college students to read a short story by Franz Kafka, one of the masters of surreal 'Kafkaesque' story-telling.

From the N.Y. Times: "After the story, the students studied a series of 45 strings of 6 to 9 letters, like 'X, M, X, R, T, V.' They later took a test on the letter strings, choosing those they thought they had seen before from a list of 60 such strings. In fact the letters were related, in a very subtle way, with some more likely to appear before or after others. The test is a standard measure of what researchers call implicit learning: knowledge gained without awareness. The students had no idea what patterns their brain was sensing or how well they were performing. But perform they did. They chose about 30 percent more of the letter strings, and were almost twice as accurate in their choices, than a comparison group of 20 students who had read a different short story, a coherent one."

The study suggests that 'nonsense' motivates our brain to try to figure out logical patterns it would otherwise miss, not just in language, but in math and in aural or visual experiences as well. Whether this is because the brain works harder to make sense of the nonsense, or for some other reason, remains to be seen.

It is a far, far better thing to have a firm anchor in nonsense than to put out on the troubled seas of thought. -John Kenneth Galbraith

Writing Practice – Nonsense Makes Us Smarter

Write a short story using fifty percent nonsense words, but so that the mood feels coherent. Write it so that it's absolutely believable—meaning grammar, punctuation, etc, is accurate. Remember Lewis Carroll's 'Jabberwocky'? "'Twas brillig and the slithy toves" makes perfect sense to us, even though the words themselves can't be translated.

Forgive me my nonsense, as I also forgive the nonsense of those that think they talk sense. -Robert Frost

Daily Happinesses

frost on the ground
the warmth of the Caribbean Sea
good deeds
using mirrors to make a room bigger and brighter
strength of purpose
lying under a coconut tree on a sunny beach
the marsh in the forest blue with bluebells

WEEK 20

You are as young as your faith, as old as your doubt; as young as your self-confidence, as old as your fear; as young as your hope, as old as your despair. –Douglas MacArthur

What is your internal age?

When my daughter was seventeen, and I was in my late forties, she remarked how sad it must be to grow old (she was focusing primarily on externals). I protested vehemently and pointed out that the view one has from a lifetime of experience makes all the difference in living. "You were cute as a button when you were seven years old; but would you want to still be seven now?" I asked. She shook her head.

"Well, that's how little I want to be seventeen now that I'm forty-seven."

That same week my mother, who had just turned 80, gave me one of her sharp, seemingly out-of-the-blue injunctions about life. She was talking about the ocean, and the rosemary growing in the yard, and the latte she'd had for breakfast, and suddenly she exclaimed: "Live a long time! It makes all the difference."

The fact is that an experience seen through the eyes of different ages is distinctive. Christopher Isherwood expressed the idea that every human being has an interior age that they fundamentally 'are' no matter what their biological age. Mine is definitely fifty or a bit more. Even when I was a teenager I remember thinking that when I was fifty I would understand something; I would know something true about life. Self-fulfilling prophecy? Perhaps.

I was at a poetry reading the other day, and a celebrated 92-year-old poet was asked whether living so long was a curse or a blessing. The question seemed to startle him, and then he hesitatingly replied, "Maybe a little of both."

What's your interior age? One way to discover it is by working on this next writing practice.

Everyone is the age of their heart. -Guatemalan Proverb

Writing Practice – What is your internal age?

Write a scene that describes: a house, two or three people, and a trip that is about to happen. Use details in your description, including furniture, weather, clothing. Try to avoid 'feeling' (in other words, don't say: "I felt sad at saying goodbye to the old dining table." Instead try: "The polished dining room table seemed blurry and I realized I was trying not to cry.") Write the scene from the point of view of the age you're at now. Take your time. This may turn out to be a fine short story.

Now describe exactly the same scene, but from the point of view of a young child. Use different vocabulary: shorter words, less interpretation about what's going on. Perhaps the description will evoke more excitement ("the dining table was piled high with all kinds of thrilling things: toothbrushes, hairbrushes, snacks for the car, books to read…") or a fog of misery (I sat at the dining table and waited, knowing they wanted me out of the way…)

And now—yes, you guessed it: exactly the same scene from the point of view of someone at a different age. Try them all: adolescence, heading off to a nursing home in old age, an adventurous sixty-year-old. Write one dozen pages in all: the same description/story written from the point of view of twelve different ages: (around) 5, 15, 25, 35, 45, 55, 65, 75, 85. 95, 105, 115.

When you're done, you'll be absolutely clear about which one flowed the most easily. That's your interior age, but it doesn't mean you have to stay there. It means that's the one you relate to, where you're most comfortable. So don't get stuck there; instead go back in your memory and see what happened around that time. If you can access that particular 'feeling' again, you'll find you can always feel good about yourself—no matter what your age.

A man's age is something impressive, it sums up his life: maturity reached slowly and against many obstacles, illnesses cured, griefs and despairs overcome, and unconscious risks taken; maturity formed through so many desires, hopes, regrets, forgotten things, loves. A man's age represents a fine cargo of experiences and memories. –Antoine de Saint-Exupéry

Daily Happinesses

talking about politics with a friend
the warm night air when you emerge from the airport
traveling light
using the right words
that moment at Joshua Tree
driving along the coast in a convertible
dancing in the gazebo after everyone else has left

WEEK 21

For the sense of smell, almost more than any other, has the power to recall memories and it is a pity that we use it so little. -Rachel Carson

The Nose Knows

Your sense of smell is possibly the oldest of the five primary senses, and associated with the formation of memories. Olfaction—the sense of smell—is handled by the same part of the brain (the limbic system) that handles memories and emotions. In the old days (a million years ago), olfaction was crucial to forming our experience of food and sex; but by now it's evolved to an art of perfumes and fragrances.

An interesting study was done several years ago: A young girl who was severely afflicted with lupus was being harmed by a medication that was curing the lupus. A physician had an interesting proposal: every time the girl took the medication that cured the lupus, he had her smell a distinct (not necessarily pleasant) fragrance. Over the course of a year, he gradually decreased the amount of the medication he was giving his patient, but continued to administer the fragrance. Amazingly, the girl's health continued to improve, as though she were taking the medication itself. But—no side effects!

This experiment made me think about how sensitive we are to the sense of smell, and it inspired in me a strong interest in aromatherapy. An aroma can evoke various moods, bringing us into harmony with our inner nature, as well as sharpening our awareness of other people and places. Usually, odor either attracts or repels. Did you know that no two people have the same personal odor—and that your odor can change simply because of your mood—or even because of a change in the weather?

Your odor memories tend to be emotional in nature, and immediately make you 'feel' good or bad, depending on whether you're remembering a positive or negative experience. That's because the sense of smell is experienced in the same part of the brain that handles memories and emotions. You recognize and respond to smells from childhood, such as the smell of fresh strawberries, your grandmother's perfume, or a new car, even though you can't necessarily identify the odor itself. Smells often bring up powerful feelings, and you may not know why.

When I read many fellow writers' blogs, I see that they often list musical numbers that they listen to for inspiration. Romance writers are listening to romantic tunes, and suspense writers are listening to something more edgy…

But what about using fragrance for inspiration? Fragrances have mood-enhancing qualities that can be just as—or more!—potent than the sound of music.

Memories, imagination, old sentiments, and associations are more readily reached through the sense of smell than through any other channel. -Oliver Wendell Holmes

Writing Practice – Inspired by Fragrance

During the next seven days choose a different scent to write with. Use these remarkable fragrances for inspiration and pleasure. Here are some suggestions—or discover your own favorites.

Are you trying to plot your story? Patchouli can be grounding and clarifying:

*"**Patchouli** has a strong, earthy, exotic aroma that eradicates nervousness and depression by putting problems into perspective. Use it help to release pent-up emotions and to see things more clearly. Its warm nature sedates and calms you; or if you're feeling dreamy and detached it will ground and integrate your physical and spiritual paths. Mysterious and exotic, this earthy, balancing essential oil evokes feelings of freedom and rebellion."**

Is one of your characters very young? Wild orange will remind you what it's like to think as a child:

*"The essential oil of **Wild Orange** has a calming effect that radiates out from the seat of your solar plexus. Long held to be a symbol of both innocence and fertility, it is a favorite among children and at weddings. It is an oil of sunshine and summer, and instills lightheartedness, warmth, and happiness. Use it to strengthen your heart and soul; it is the perfect oil for when you take things too seriously and forget to laugh."*

If you're writing a tense, difficult scene in your story, try fennel:

*"With its powerful effect on your heart, **Fennel** offers you strength and endurance in times of hardship. It helps you become*

aware of all the extraneous excesses in your life, and heightens your appreciation for what is essential. Its nature is to restore inner clarity. Fennel has a long history of use as a medicine and a culinary aid in both Western and Eastern cultures. The Ancient Egyptians used it for various ailments, and the early Greek athletes ate the seeds to increase their strength while training for Olympic games. The Romans believed it gave them stamina and courage."

To try to see a situation from a man's point of view:

"Cumin's *spicy, penetrating, and pungent aroma has a stimulating effect on your emotions. Used in perfumes, love potions, and baths for its aphrodisiac effect, especially for men, it has also been held in high esteem since Biblical times mainly for its digestive properties. The Hindus saw it as a symbol of fidelity. It was also highly regarded in Britain during the Middle Ages when it was used as currency. The word cumin is derived from the Persian city Kerman, where most cumin was produced."*

Are you writing a sexy romantic scene? Get out your ylang.

"Use exotic, sensual ***Ylang*** *both to entice and to relax. Its intense sweet floral fragrance builds confidence and removes fear or anxiety. The name means "flower of flowers," and it can be intoxicating and hypnotic. Ylang has a long-standing reputation as potent aphrodisiac, and you can also use it to relieve stress, irritation, impatience, or anxiety, for it calms and nourishes your heart."*

Are you one of those writers who get their best ideas while asleep? Try Mimosa.

*"**Mimosa's** nurturing qualities appease your worries, fears, and over-sensitivity. Its gentle embrace will lift your spirits to a state of inner repose. It interfaces well with your subconscious mind, enhancing psychic awareness during dreams and visualizations. Use it before going to sleep to induce amazing visions. It will remind you to love—and to truly live your dreams."*

Today, do you just want to experience happiness?

*"A mere breath of the sweet aroma of **Jasmine** can change your emotions profoundly, lifting you from despair or depression into a realm of calm optimism, self-confidence, and happiness. Native to Persia and Kashmir, yasmin means "Gift from God." In Sufi poetry, Jasmine was used as a symbol of love and spiritual longing. Ruled by Isis, the goddess of the moon, Jasmine can help you become aware of your hidden passions and desires and show you ways to you deal with dilemmas in relationships. Use it to deepen your intuition and insight, and to bring you feelings of pleasure and euphoria."*

*All these excerpts are from *Heaven Falls* by Winslow Eliot, published by Telemachus Press in 2010.

Daily Happinesses

being given a bouquet of yellow daffodils during a snowstorm
a moment of self-confidence
magic spells
swimming with sea turtles
stepping into the mirror and looking around
vast distances

June

Week 22 – Why I dance
Week 23 – Men and women
Week 24 – Sitting is deadly
Week 25 – Satisfying conclusions
Week 26 – When you come to the end of a rope

WEEK 22

I would believe only in a God that knows how to dance. –Friedrich Nietzsche

Why I Dance

One of the most well-known cards of the Tarot is the Magician, or the Juggler. Every esoteric path begins with the Magician, who teaches that what is essential in the beginning of any journey is learning to accomplish the task at hand with effortless concentration. This effortless concentration, or 'flow,' is described by author Mihaly Csikszentmihaly as "being completely involved in an activity for its own sake. The ego falls away. Time flies. Every action, movement, and thought follows inevitably from the previous one, like playing jazz. Your whole being is involved, and you're using your skills to the utmost."

An artist like Din Yanyong, for instance, studied for many years how to draw and paint detailed still-lifes and animals. Eventually, he could draw a picture of a horse using only one line.

For a pianist, the effortless concentration comes from thousands of hours of practicing scales over and over, until one's fingers are one with the piano. It's then that one can freely play.

The poet Robert Frost wrote "Stopping by the Woods on Snowy Evening" after having stayed up one summer night writing a long—and forgettable—poem called "New Hampshire." Exhausted, he went outside and saw the sun rising, and was suddenly inspired to write a poem "about the snowy evening and the little horse as if I'd had a hallucination in just a few minutes without strain."

For a writer, after mastery of the craft has been achieved, the concentration without effort often comes from letting go. We are too much in our heads, and when we turn off the switch and simply let go, extraordinary things can happen.

But letting go may be the hardest practice.

One excellent method to help you achieve this is to dance. Seriously. It's transforming work into play, which is part of the secret of flow. For me, sufi dance—or all middle eastern dancing, for that matter!—is the way I release and join with the flow that tends to get clogged in my writing. There is nothing more transporting than to move to the yearning notes from the ney, the rich strumming of the oud, the resounding zills and darbuka. Whether intensely rhythmic, sorrowful, joyful, profound, the melodies and voices weave through my heart like syrup—sweetening, energizing—and take me out of myself.

The music that moves me may not be the music that moves you. Although I admit I dance to just about anything: Celtic folk songs, Motown, the mournful Japanese koto, African drums, Brazilian samba, Hawaiian hula… you'll need to choose the sounds that draw out your imagination, as well as getting your toes to tap. It's not just about your body moving, but your heart moving as well.

Here's a poem by Rumi:

Dance, when you're broken open.
Dance, if you've torn the bandage off.
Dance in the middle of the fighting.
Dance in your blood.
Dance, when you're perfectly free.

Writing Practice – Dance

Yes, *dance.*

Schedule an hour for this. Close the door, turn off the phone, and don't allow any interruption. Dance the whole time. Sometimes when we used to dance in Stephanie Forest's legendary classes, much of the dance class was spent lying down with our eyes closed. Sometimes only our hands moved. Still, it was all dancing.

The important thing is to listen, and to let your mind and body be carried by the music. Let your breathing breathe itself, let your body move by itself.

You'll find, at the end of the hour, that you have a whole new 'flow' to your state of being. Dancing reminds you that there's no separation between mind and body, and the energy that is released is indeed effortless. We tend to focus too much in our heads when we write, and that can create frustration and blockage. Dancing frees us. Even better, it teaches us to transform work into play, to make things easy and light. Writing is a joy.

This week's task is to enter a state of concentration without effort, where you as a writer become one with your inner self, your pen, your time and space, and the words you write. It's to recognize this truth: when you're in the flow, it's all one.

Even after your hour is up, try to dance as you wash the dishes, dance as you head into the classroom, and dance while you're talking on the phone or filling your car with gas.

How can we know the dancer from the dance? –William Butler Yeats

Daily Happinesses

fresh stuffed grape leaves with lemon
sitting under a palm tree
finding the old woman in the hut and asking the question
swimming at Swift's Beach
getting dressed for the ball
low summer stars
a tree that blooms diamonds

WEEK 23

Well, there's a little bit of man in every woman and a little bit of woman in every man. –Betty Smith, *A Tree Grows in Brooklyn*

Men and Women

A long time ago someone (a man) read a book I wrote and was startled into saying, "Wow! You write like a man!"

He meant it as a compliment.

I thought a lot about this.

Did you know that Charles Dickens, in 1858, wrote to a friend thusly about George Eliot's *Scenes of Clerical Life*: "...whose first stories I can never say enough of, I think them so truly admirable. But, if those two volumes, or a part of them, were not written by a woman—then should I begin to believe that I am a woman myself."

What in George Eliot's writing made it utterly obvious to Mr. Dickens that she was a woman, in spite of her pseudonym? What did the friend who read my book mean when he said that "I wrote like a man"?

I'll suggest two things, and then you can add some more, since this discussion is ongoing and forever. Very broadly, then:

One important difference can be seen in a man's brevity in thinking, compared to a woman's. A man thinks thoughts sharply, and linearly, and he usually writes like that. A character goes from A to B, and even if there is lengthy description or heartache involved, it is presented in a slightly detached, action-oriented way. Women writers, on the other hand, work a lot more with internal dialog. We tend to prefer novels in which the characters' inner world is constantly described. Hardly anything has to happen, as long as a lot happens on the inside.

That novel I wrote long ago (called The Director, and it was never published) was lauded by my male friends and ho-hummed by my women friends. I was experimenting with a different way of writing, one in which I hoped the action would speak louder than words. I used a phrase like this:

She stared. Then she stood abruptly and left the table.

Not: *She stared. Was this all that was left? One moment they meant the world to each other, and the next he was cutting the ties between them forever. She rose, not knowing what to say.*

What could she say? Was there anything that could make a difference? Etc., etc.

See what I mean?

Another difference is how a man and a woman relate to their characters and scenes. I'll never forget a woman critic asking me, "Do you really like Jonny [my central character]?" I realized that I admired him, enjoyed writing and developing him, but I was not 'in love' with him. I wasn't crazy about him, the way I fall madly in love with the heroes of my romantic novels.

But male authors, you can be sure, would never gushily admit to falling in love with their protagonists. They are more likely to admire, or perhaps wish they were like them. Sometimes I almost sense a friendly competitiveness between author and protagonist, an affectionate punch on the arm, one of those look-you-in-the-eye kind of manly moments.

If the world were a logical place, men would ride side saddle. -Rita Mae Brown

Writing Practice – Men and Women

This week's writing practice follows on this musing. For those of you who are poets, you can create this in poetic form.

You are walking along a narrow road that widens on to a beach. Describe this beach from the point of view of a man.

Use a lot of detail, but every detail has to create a feeling about the man who is approaching the beach. Write no more than one or two paragraphs, and do not use dialog or action! Don't say, "I felt peaceful looking at the waves." No, no. Say, "the waves barely seemed to move, lulled to peacefulness by the late afternoon stillness..." Or, "The topless babes lying there looked hot. Sweat trickled from under my arms."

Only use description for this exercise; and remember to access all five senses.

Now describe exactly the same beach from the point of view of a woman. How would a woman experience the peacefulness of the ocean? Perhaps she wants to dip her toe in and sees the flash of her freshly polished red toenail in the sea-green foam. Perhaps she raises her fingertips to the sky and stretches, breathing in the scent of the waves. Her thoughts would be more stream-like and swift.

The two points of view—male and female—need to be completely clear to the reader, simply from how the beach is described.

I never hated a man enough to give him his diamonds back. –Zsa Zsa Gabor

Daily Happinesses

going through old photographs
personalizing a new computer
planning a trip to the south seas
anticipating the wedding party
dried leaves falling slowly in a still afternoon
a tiny kitten sleeping on your chest
thinking about mysteries

WEEK 24

Gardens are not made by singing 'Oh, how beautiful,' and sitting in the shade. –Rudyard Kipling

Sitting is Deadly

Scientists have discovered something new! ***Sitting is deadly.*** Spending most of your days with most of your weight resting on your delicate lower spine is dangerous, even if you regularly exercise.

Apparently, after just a few hours of sitting, the body starts sending hazardous warning signals to your brain (like telling genes that regulate the glucose in your body to shut down). Even for people who exercise, spending long stretches of time just sitting is still terribly risky. One article I read stated that a scientist had pointed out the lethal effects of sitting in research studies over fifty years ago. (His findings were allegedly suppressed by the powerful chair lobby.)

For most people, Writing is imagined to be the process of being hunched over a desk and applying pen to paper or fingerpads to keyboards. When I'm asked whether I 'worked' today, usually the question refers to how many hours I sat in a chair at my desk.

Now we're told that using a stool to lean on, so more weight is on your legs, or stretching out on a chaise lounge, is much healthier than sitting at a desk. In fact, it might even save your life.

If we bring these fascinating scientific findings into the classroom, we realize that allowing children to put their feet on their desks, to fidget as much as possible, to stretch out on the floor or to get up and walk around whenever they're inclined, will improve concentration, increase productivity, and lead to much better overall physical health.

Habits are at first cobwebs, then cables. –Spanish Proverb

Writing Practice – Break your habits

Write somewhere new. Even if the desk and chair routine is working for you, try a shady hammock for a change, or lying on your stomach. Or try writing while you're standing—you might find yourself gesturing madly and even reading dialog out loud.

Break another habit—not just the position you're in when you write. For example, try using a pen to write. Or if you always write things in long hand, try typing a first draft. If you always have coffee when you write, try a glass of water or some lemonade. If you need people around you, and you always head out to the local coffee shop, try writing in a room alone. And if you think the idea of writing with lots of people around is outrageous and you would hate it—then try that experience.

Habit is habit, and not to be flung out of the window by any man, but coaxed downstairs a step at a time. –Mark Twain

Daily Happinesses

purple and green
being held all night long
gardening in the light rain
sitting around the table
late afternoon in an almost-deserted town
the stillness of contemplation
seizing the day

WEEK 25

Great is the art of beginning, but greater is the art of ending. –Henry Wadsworth Longfellow

Satisfying Conclusions

I love conclusions. I remember a friend saying that she dreaded coming to the final chapters of a novel because she couldn't bear the story to end. I'm the opposite: I love the moment the story draws to a close; the conflict over; the exhausting seeking ended; the relationship resolved; the tears drying; the murderer found…

Even in expository or other non-fiction writing I enjoy coming to the end more than I enjoy savoring each sentence and mulling over concepts. Most of the time, I'd rather the imagery and ideas be summarized. This is partly because I'm a fast, impatient reader. I tend to grasp concepts quickly, and think I understand more than I actually do. I try to slow down by reading stories and books that intrigue me—usually history or philosophy. Still, the conclusion is where I land most happily.

I think the purpose of a good conclusion is to give every reader with a fulfilled sense of satisfaction.

A conclusion is the writer's bridge to the reader's own life. If you haven't in some way grabbed the reader by the lapels and connected with them, either through ideas, emotional content, character, or intriguing thought, then you've missed an opportunity. The conclusion needs to remind readers that they and you are connected, even if it's by briefly taking them back over the story or the essay they just read.

Your conclusion can be more creative than you realize. Don't just repeat the thesis statement or end with the classic fairy-tale line of "They lived happily ever after." For example, after a couple of years of romantic, political, and social intrigue, the lovable Phineas Finn in Anthony Trollope's eponymous novel is forced to return home to Ireland and his abandoned fiancée. She has no clue of the depth of passion and ambition Phineas has experienced, but the reader has, and really doesn't know how he will tolerate the peace, poverty, and boredom of going back home to a pretty, witless young girl. But at the very end of the novel, because of the friends he made while in high places, he gets offered a fairly good job with a decent salary, and he realizes nothing can prevent his marriage any longer:

> *"But I have been making up my mind to wait ever so long," said Mary.*
>
> *"Then your mind must be unmade," said Phineas.*
>
> *What was the nature of the reply to Lord Cantrip the reader may imagine, and thus we will leave our hero an Inspector of the Poor Houses in the County of Cork.*

Although you can't introduce a new topic, or characters, or concepts in the conclusion, you can push your way into a broader view of an issue, or point out why the purport of your story or essay matters. Here's the end of *The Proud Tower*, a history by one of the greatest writers of history of all time, Barbara Tuchman: *The proud tower built up through the great age of European civilization was an edifice of grandeur and passion, of riches and beauty, and dark reliance, more confidence, more hope; greater magnificence, extravagance and elegance; more careless ease, more gaiety, more pleasure in each other's company and conversation, more injustice and hypocrisy, more misery and want, more sentiment including false sentiment, less sufferance of mediocrity, more dignity in work, more delight in nature, more zest. The Old World had much that has since been lost, whatever may have been gained. Looking back on it from 1915, Emile Verhaeren, the Belgian Socialist poet, dedicated his pages, "With emotion, to the man I used to be."*

You almost don't have to read the book to know what it was all about!

Here's another one that takes my breath away with its incisive conclusion of one of the most profound explorations of the essence of poetry and meaning: *Poetic Diction* by Owen Barfield: *Yet all conclusions of this nature could be no more than subjective shadows of the forces themselves, of the two living realities, which can actually be known, once our intellect has brought us to the point of looking out for them; being themselves neither subjective nor objective, but as concrete and self-sustaining in every way as the Sun and the Moon – which may well be their proper names.*

Did you read *Three Men in a Boat* by Jerome K. Jerome? What a hilarious adventure down the Thames that was, that ends thus:

"Well," said Harris, reaching his hand out for his glass, "we have had a pleasant trip, and my hearty thanks for it to old Father Thames – but I think we did well to chuck it when we did. Here's to Three Men well out of a Boat!"

And Montmorency, standing on his hind legs before the window, peering out into the night, gave a short bark of decided concurrence with the toast.

As I said earlier, your conclusion should leave your reader feeling satisfied and glad that they read all the way to the end. So that's the concept behind conclusions—now for the how-to. Here are some suggestions for writing an appealing conclusion:

- Refer to the introductory paragraph or to the basic theme of your story.
- End with a provocative insight or intriguing quotation.
- Inspire a course of action, a solution to an issue, or a suggestion.
- Point out possible consequences, or even end with a moral or a warning.
- Evoke vivid imagery.
- Futurize—describe how the events made a difference.

Try NOT to:

- End with the same thesis statement you started out with, without using what you built on in the essay to expand on it. Worse: don't state your thesis for the first time in the conclusion.
- Introduce a new idea or subtopic; and do not introduce a new storyline or character in the final paragraph.

- Don't apologize: "I'm not an expert, but…" or "Others may disagree with me, but…"
- In fact, needless to say, avoid all unnecessary fluff, like: "in conclusion" or "in summary."
- Attempt to make up for a thin storyline or an incomplete essay by cramming in too much information at the end.
- Make emotional appeals that have not been established earlier.
- Include information that should be in the story or paper.

Murder will out, this my conclusion. -Geoffrey Chaucer

Writing practice – Conclusion

Write a one-paragraph conclusion to a story that you haven't written. You'll need to resolve the story you've imagined. Without reiterating the tale, or summarizing, you need to make the gist of the tale clear. If you would rather play around, write the conclusion to an expository essay that you have NOT written. For example, you could write a concluding paragraph for a mythical essay on "Tact." Here's an example of a simple conclusion:

"If she had spoken gently to her cousin, they might still be friends. Even when speaking the truth, using tact makes a huge difference."

As always, try doing this exercise daily for a week—concluding a different story or essay each day. You'll be amazed how much easier it gets as you loosen up your conclusion-writing muscles and start to enjoy the freedom of concluding a story without worrying how you got there. It can be a lot of fun.

There are some days when I think I'm going to die from an overdose of satisfaction. –Salvador Dali

Daily Happinesses

Tahitian gardenias in moonlight
the cricket explaining things
sunset over the mountain range and the valley darkening
rain after intense, hot sorrow
good newspaper stories
touching old amber
a unicorn in the garden

WEEK 26

Some of us think holding on makes us strong;
but sometimes it is letting go. –Hermann Hesse

When You Come to the End of a Rope

A long time ago, during a low point in my life, someone tried to advise me: "When you come to the end of a rope, tie a knot and hang on." I remember snapping back: "When you come to the end of a rope, you should let it go and find another one!"

We are all hanging onto ropes throughout our lives, and it is sometimes one of the scariest things in the world to let them go.

One of my ropes, for example, was that from the time I was in my early teens I wanted to be a published author. I held onto that rope through adolescence, into college, and when I moved to New York City in my twenties when I did, finally, get my first book contract. But when I wasn't being published by a mainstream publishing house, I tended to feel bereft, a failure, a nonentity. It became almost like an addiction: I *had* to be published, and frequently, to feel normal.

Letting go felt impossible until a few years ago. There were a lot of factors, but the main one had to do with author John P. Locke. I did some editing on one of his novels, and over the course of the next few months, we became friends.

From him, I re-learned a key element to my own writing process that I had forgotten: Writing is *fun*.

John didn't say this out loud: I got it because of who he is and how he communicates and writes. When we wrote to each other, everything seemed easier and more lighthearted. There was definitely a 'flow' in his writing that inspired me, simply because of his attitude toward his own writing. When I first read John's novels, I recognized in them the quality of a really fine writer. His style is fast and furious, hilarious, descriptive, violent. From the first few pages of *Lethal People*, I knew that, if he wanted to, he could be published by a Major Publishing House.

To my fascination, John had no interest in mainstream publishing. The idea of months or years of querying agents, then more months or years of an agent trolling a novel through the snobbish bowels of mainstream publishing houses, and the peculiar desire to receive rejection letters, meant nothing to him. He wanted to self-publish. He wanted his books out and available *now*, with a cover he liked, blurbs and ads and press releases that he approved, interviews and reviews by people who were appreciative, and a writing-and-publishing process that he *enjoyed*.

John writes because it's FUN.

When we met, I had forgotten that feeling. How novels used to pour from me, with cheerful abundance, like a fountain. How words were playful, interesting things—not heavy stones to build a tome. Sentences could come and go, like a breeze. Chapters were filled with laughter and (usually) lots of kisses. A story was light as sunshine, and sprang forth like flowers.

In addition to John Locke, I have one other person to thank for helping me to let go of an old rope that was exhausting me by holding onto it. That person is Claudia Jackson. Claudia was a pioneer in the independent publishing movement. She began a small company—Telemachus Press—to publish her husband's book, and she was willing to take on my novels when I asked. She produced beautiful, professional, high-caliber books for me, and held my hand as we navigated the shoals of distribution and promotion. Her title in the company was and is the "promise keeper"—and she has never let me down. I was very lucky to have two such great companions to catch me when I let go of my old, worn-out rope!

Thanks to John Locke and Claudia Jackson, I was finally able to let go of a rope I'd clung to for far too long. Since then, I've found that I can sit back and watch in wonder as one sentence leads mysteriously to the next, and stories grow of their own accord—because it's 'flow'—because it's fun.

Try to bring a sense of fun back into your writing life. Imagine the process as an adventure, a party, or a rest—whatever you like best.

You can only lose what you cling to. –Buddha

Writing Practice – Letting Go

Think of a 'rope' in your life that you're hanging on to. It can be a big rope—like a job you're not happy with but feel you have to stay with, or a relationship that perhaps is nearing its end. Or it can be tiny—like a sock you'll never finish knitting or a haiku that isn't working. Imagine how tired your arms are, how exhausted you feel, how you long for someone to come and help you back up the rope to where you were. Feel your loneliness: there's only you there, hanging on to that rope, legs dangling over the abyss. Maybe even cry a bit.

Now, instead of trying to climb back up the rope, imagine letting go. You realize that to hang on to a rope when your arms are aching is just plain silly. There's no danger—everything around is soft and slow and warm and lovely. You're tumbling gently through a safe, interesting world that is totally unexpected, but still your very own, because it's your own creation. Think Alice's rabbit hole adventure, for example.

Close your eyes and allow the best experience imaginable to come to you—don't try to force it. You might find yourself with a whole new way of looking at something that you were previously stuck on.

Now write it down. First, describe the rope you've been holding onto and the misery and ache you feel. Then describe the wonder of what occurs when you let go of the rope. Think outside the box—in fact, maybe nothing happens at all. Maybe everything that you were afraid would happen when you let go disappears.

Maybe you simply feel relief.

When I let go of what I am, I become what I might be." –Lao-Tzu

Daily Happinesses

a fresh cord of wood delivered
intrigue
a wide-brimmed turquoise sun hat
castles in Bavaria
the eye of love
passing the peace pipe
snuggling together

WINSLOW ELIOT
WriteSpa
Writing through the year . . .

July

Week 27 – Stream of consciousness
Week 28 – Do nothing
Week 29 – Why I love fiction
Week 30 – There are no words for it

WEEK 27

One writes… not out of the leaves of trees still to be observed, nor by means of botany and soil-science; but it grows like a seed in the dark out of the leaf-mold of the mind: out of all that has been seen or thought or read, that has long ago been forgotten, descending into the deeps. No doubt there is much personal selection, as with a gardener: what one throws on one's personal compost-heap; and my mold is evidently made largely of linguistic matter. –J. R. R. Tolkien

Stream of consciousness

Deep thinking, rich feeling, and drowsy summer afternoons are not incompatible. If you practice all three, they become a particularly intriguing stream of consciousness in your writing.

What is stream of consciousness? Basically, it's eavesdropping on the heart and mind of a character—being privy to his or her innermost private thoughts. By writing in this style, we're exposing the most intimate qualities of a human being, ones that we are hardly aware of even in ourselves. After all, how often do we think about what we are thinking about?

William James defined four aspects of consciousness, which I loosely interpret thus:

- deeply personal, individual
- always changing
- never ceasing
- interested in some things to the exclusion of others; all the time making choices about what to be conscious of

These are all important, but the last, to us writers, is the most fascinating. Why do we glom onto the little red wagon in that particular poem or the sound of the rooster crowing in our story? There are at least a hundred other experiences on the fringe of our consciousness that we could have chosen instead. What we decide to leave out of our story is as important as what we include.

The streams of images, thoughts, and emotions that flow when we write this way are not mere shattered fragments. They are windows into the heart of the character we describe. We're taking our reader on an interior journey, one that synthesizes the experience of weather, or horror, or love with the person experiencing it, rather than the old-fashioned style of writing which was more analytic or descriptive.

The task is not to write about a 'real' world, but rather to synthesize experiences, pain and suffering, and ideas with a world that doesn't really make much sense. Face it—there's an awful lot of unexplainable mystery going on all around us, all the time. What is life? What is your purpose? Where does the universe begin or end? And on and on. Writing from the heart of a character in this way brings us back to a sense of one-ness, with others, and with the world itself. There is no longer the separation of object–subject, or "I and thou." We are actually creating ourselves, as much as we create characters, countries, and stories. And perhaps that is as much as we can understand about life anyway.

So this week write as you are buoyed by wild thyme and forget-me-nots, in the shade of a thickly branching maple. The brimful bubbling noises of the brook. It's at the bend in the river that the world began. Sandcastles and red pails—Ella calling from the ice cream truck. The branches sway. Somber telegram. Oh, there's a robin! And then that boy kissed me—he had fond eyes, but fond of what? We were in the barn and had lost the others. The bobolink singing its heart out—a cherry pie and my mother is still around. I think we've heard that song before; the stars seem extra big tonight. A long boat ride to the island. Dancing with my father to Benny Goodman, and the notes were all silver and streamy. Sometimes, somewhere, the sun doesn't set. That was a good voyage, the sea met the sky and salt crystals on soft decks.

Be who you are and say what you feel, because those who mind don't matter and those who matter don't mind. –Dr. Seuss

Writing Practice – Where Did I Come From, Who Am I, Where Am I Going?

Try writing an autobiographical piece about yourself. Write it in the third person, as a short story, with interior dialog, description, mood—all the qualities of writing we've been working on over these past months.

What is most important about your life? Birth date, hair color, job? Or is it a formative experience? Or might it be something you believe in?

Close your eyes and really think about this: What do you want people to know about you?

Come up with an over-arching theme rather than a time-line of your life. What inspired you to leave your home or to sing in that first coffee house? What is a secret longing you've never shared? Your theme might be a great obstacle, a true love, the onslaught of sickness, impending doom, joy, a sea change. As you write, locate what the theme of your biography is, and when you title your piece, try to net that theme in the title and, perhaps, a subtitle.

When a biography is written in a fictional style, where the reader is allowed a deep glimpse into the subject's head and heart, it works much more powerfully. If you're stuck on how to begin, mull on Paul Gaugin's famous painting. In it, he asks the vital questions that we need to ask of our friends, as well as of ourselves:

WHERE DID WE COME FROM
WHO ARE WE
WHERE ARE WE GOING
P. Gaugin 1897 Tahiti

After you've mulled, using stream of consciousness, write three paragraphs that describe your life. But only use summary analogies or memories or metaphors. Don't attend to grammar, spelling, punctuation—unless it's for artistic or poetic reasons. For example, during one class, a student wrote about a depressed time by describing the rain on window pains. That works! You can even make up words that sound like what you are trying to express. Or try just using verbs—or turning every word in your piece into a verb as you write.

Do this same exercise every day this week, and see how differently your autobiography emerges in each one.

Use this writing method to free up those writing muscles. When you exercise, you strengthen and shorten a muscle, and that's why it's important to stretch and flex before and after. So start writing at the bottom of the page and work your way up. Or begin at the end of the notebook, or turn it upside down. Write in different shapes each day, or use bubbles for each phrase. Or create a sun in the center of the page and have words and images raying outward. Use colored pencils and be random and creative: Don't always use red if you're recalling an angry or passionate mood. What does it feel like if you use green or a peaceful blue?

Sometimes your piece of writing will be tinged by a mood of nostalgia.

At other times you'll experience bliss.

Still other times you'll recall the thrill of discovery or meeting a person...

See if you can latch onto a theme or mood as you let your mind stream through your past and cull imagery and feeling, and, in an abbreviated version, tell your life story.

To be nobody but yourself in a world which is doing its best, night and day, to make you everybody else means to fight the hardest battle which any human being can fight; and never stop fighting. –e.e. cummings

Daily Happinesses

the tiger stalking through the jungle
painting the barn
staying up all night talking
dancing in your sleep
looking out a train window
eating ice cream during the short, hot night
discovering the underwater cave

WEEK 28

Do Nothing

A perfect summer day is when the sun is shining, the breeze is blowing, the birds are singing, and the lawn mower is broken. -James Den

Did you know that for about a third of our waking day our minds are lost in a world that has little or nothing to do with the task at hand? That's about five hours a day of daydreaming, and, if that's really the case, I figure it had better be good for us.

Interestingly, neuroscientists describe our brain as having two separate 'networks': an administrative network, which we use when we're busy accomplishing a task, and a default network, which is the one that we automatically revert to when we're at rest or not concentrating on something—for example, if we're watching television. In other words, the default network 'switches off' when we need to focus. And when one network is 'lit up,' the other is not.

However—and this is the splendid part—when we daydream, *both* networks are lit up at the same time.

Neuroscientists have determined that when the mind is at rest, it is actually more active (in a good way!) than when it is engaged in a task.

"Many neuroscientists have long assumed that much of the neural activity inside your head when at rest matches your subdued, somnolent mood. In this view, the activity in the resting brain represents nothing more than random noise, akin to the snowy pattern on the television screen when a station is not broadcasting. But recent analysis produced by neuroimaging technologies has revealed something quite remarkable: a great deal of meaningful activity is occurring in the brain when a person is sitting back and doing nothing at all.

"It turns out that when your mind is at rest—when you are daydreaming quietly in a chair, say, [or] asleep in a bed or anesthetized for surgery—dispersed brain areas are chattering away to one another. And the energy consumed by this ever active messaging, known as the brain's default mode, is about 20 times that used by the brain when it responds consciously to an outside stimulus. Indeed, most things we do consciously, be it sitting down to eat dinner or making a speech, mark a departure from the baseline activity of the brain default mode." (Marcus E. Raichle, "The Brain's Dark Energy," Scientific American, March 2010.)

There are lots of theories as to why this may be so, but nothing conclusive, except this: people who are prone to daydreaming, and whose networks are working simultaneously, score higher on creativity tests and are more able to 'think outside the box.' Research has also connected daydreaming with healthy social adaptability and improved school and work performance. One Australian researcher found that "children who don't get enough down time to daydream or who fill in their down time with too much television produce works that are "tedious and unimaginative."

Daydreaming is perhaps one of the most underrated things we all do. It's usually considered a waste of time, annoying, or even rude. It makes your parents nervous, it makes your teachers edgy. If you look up 'daydreaming' in Google, the third entry states—without controversy—that "daydreaming is a behavioral disorder." Freud claims that daydreaming is a neurosis or psychosis.

Argh.

People who know me well have had to listen to my emphatic discourse on the value of 'doing nothing' for a long time now. I've claimed—without much support—that doing nothing is a vital activity in our busy lives, not only for children but for all of us.

Most of my friends and relatives just don't get it.

'Nothing time' does not mean leisure—like zoning out with a movie or even reading a book. It means daydreaming. It means looking out the window—it even means allowing yourself to be bored. It means letting go of all those heady shoulds and musts and have-tos, and instead letting thoughts and ideas come to you. It's a time to open yourself, to find a place that is so quiet you become one with the world, without trying. There's no effort involved, just as there's no effort in the central activity of breathing.

Remember this from Winnie the Pooh?

"What I like doing best is Nothing," said Christopher Robin.

"How do you do Nothing?" asked Pooh, after he had wondered for a long time.

"Well, it's when people call out at you just as you're going off to do it, 'What are you going to do, Christopher Robin?' and you say, 'Oh, nothing,' and then you go and do it."

"Oh, I see," said Pooh.

"This is a nothing sort of thing that we're doing now."

"Oh, I see," said Pooh again.

"It means just going along, listening to all the things you can't hear, and not bothering."

"Oh!" said Pooh.

So, put down your pen or turn off your computer and look out the window. Stand under some pine trees and let your mind wander. Or sit in the shade of a taverna and nibble on olives. Or lie on the couch in your living room. Is there a beach nearby? Don't listen to the waves—let them just be. Don't talk. Forget about your word count. Don't worry. Do nothing. Turn off the telephone, hide the remote, close your journal, ignore your inbox.

See what dreams and ideas drift to you instead of your chasing after them.

Sometimes when one of my students is particularly stressed, I'll assign them this homework: "Set your timer for twenty minutes, sit in a chair or lie on a couch, and do nothing. No reading, no social media, no playing music. Nothing."

One particularly stressed student replied, "Oh, my mother won't let me do that."

I replied, "Please have her call me. I'll explain that it's your homework."

Her eyes widened. Since that time she has become a calmer, far more productive student.

So, parents, put away all those crazy toys that are supposed to stimulate your baby's mind: gazing out the window or into your loving eyes is much more productive! And parents of teens: make sure your kids' downtime is validated. And teachers—lighten up on all that homework. Sure, chores have to be done, but shift your priorities. Doing nothing is just as important as washing the dishes.

I was trying to daydream, but my mind kept wandering. –Stephen Wright

Writing Practice – Do Nothing

That's it. That's the practice. Do nothing.

Summer afternoon – summer afternoon; to me those have always been the two most beautiful words in the English language. –Henry James

Daily Happinesses

planting the daylilies
an appreciative note
dancing at an afternoon tea party
the depth of being
the owl whispering in your ear
dozing during a picnic on the castle grounds
the cactus blooming again

WEEK 29

Why I Love Fiction

All good books are alike in that they are truer than if they had really happened and after you are finished reading one you will feel that all that happened to you and afterwards it all belongs to you; the good and the bad, the ecstasy, the remorse and sorrow, the people and the places and how the weather was. If you can get so that you can give that to people, then you are a writer. -Ernest Hemingway

A phrase that troubles me when I'm giving a creative writing class is when someone blurts out about a piece of their writing: "But that really happened," or "But it's true."

When anyone says that, I get the feeling that the writer believes that real life is in some way better than fiction. They believe that if something is 'true'—in the sense that it actually occurred—the importance of the writing is elevated.

Not so!

Fiction is to non-fiction what a painting is to a snapshot. The reason fiction writing is so glorious, so universal, so powerful is that the entire human experience is elevated through story. Characters are richer and deeper because we understand their feelings and motivations. Descriptions matter more because we see not just through our own eyes, but through the eyes of an artist. Our deepest emotions are tapped and brought to life. We enter into worlds that are otherwise invisible to us. We laugh, we weep, we descend into horror, we are brought to ways of thinking we simply could not find on our own.

It always amazes me how little we know about each other. When I lived in New York City, I remember looking up at the hundreds of windows in a random apartment building and imagining the real live stories going on within each apartment. Or watching my fellow subway travelers and wondering where they came from and where they were going. Who were they going to meet? Why did that young man wear a secret smile? How did that frail old woman feel when she had to push through the crowd to emerge onto the platform? Where were those dressed-up teenagers headed and what were they whispering about?

A reason fiction is so appealing is that all those mysteries are revealed. It's an extraordinary gift to know what someone is thinking or what their motive is for their next action. Imagine sitting on a bus, and being able to 'hear' what the person next to you is contemplating. To know their story and their experience of living. Not just that, but to be included in their insight into their own thoughts. As the layers peel away, a person is revealed to us and our thirst for knowing more about them is quenched. That's why I love fiction.

It's much harder to do that in real life. When you first meet someone, it's as though physical presence and the relationship between you creates layers and distance between you. People say the human connection is the most important thing in the world, and I agree—and at the same time it fascinates me how hard it is to make that connection. We're all such insulated bubbles, caught up in our own heads and encased in private emotion. I am continually astounded when I learn something about someone I thought I knew well—a childhood experience they had, perhaps, or a feeling about something that matters to me as well, or a difficult thought.

If you read someone's journal, chances are you'll get pretty drowsy fairly quickly. But if you read a journal in novel form—that is, created as part of a story, a journey, an experience that is transformed from the personal to the archetypal, then you're hooked. You experience. You feel. You care. You think. You think anew.

> *Only in men's imagination does every truth find an effective and undeniable existence. Imagination, not invention, is the supreme master of art as of life.* -Joseph Conrad

Writing Practice – Making it up

Recall a personal, real experience you had recently and write it down as it actually happened. Contain the account within two or three pages and write it in the first person.

Now read your experience through and imagine the opposite ending to what actually happened. Rewrite the same event in the third person, with a different ending.

Read it through again. As you do, imagine a purpose or motive to the main character that is much more urgent or motivating than the initial one you wrote about. Say your experience was getting on the wrong bus when you went to work last week. Assume in real life you got off the wrong bus, got on the right one, you were late to work, and missed an important meeting.

Now, what if there turned out to be no buses headed back in the right direction? What if you ended up in a strange coffee shop in a town you'd never been to before.

Sure, you're anxious about the meeting, and that needs to be the overriding urgency to the tone of your story. You're missing the chance of a lifetime, you think. Your cell phone battery has died and when you ask if you can borrow someone else's, they look at you as though you're crazy.

What's going on?

Perhaps you're caught in a Twilight Zone experience—where any effort to find your way back to your familiar world is futile. Or perhaps you meet your soul mate or your long-lost daughter.

The wrong bus turns out to be Destiny. The people you encounter turn out to be catalysts you're finding yourself.

Create a beginning, middle, and end in your mind. You might want to make some notes.

See what happens. You're drawing on yourself and your experience, and that's important. But when you're telling a story, you're also drawing on vision, inspiration.

That's just as important. Make it up—imagine—and know that by using your imagination, you'll stop being stuck. Your imagination will set you free. You'll be able to move from the so-called 'real' into something even more sublime: Fiction.

Daily Happinesses

the color of dawn
hearing a smile in a voice on the telephone
the Moonlight Sonata
waving a wand and the house is clean
gazing into the fire and seeing a salamander
stretching your arms as high as the moon
sunlight on piles of antique stained glass

WEEK 30

There are no words for it

They say that the Sami people, who live in the land closest to the Arctic Circle, have over a thousand words for snow, but none for just 'snow'—as we refer to it. I've often felt that our word 'love' could use at least 1,000 words to replace how we generally use it, and yet the closest I've discovered for a more specific meaning is when I heard someone ask, "Do you love him or do you love-love him?"

We could do better!

And words don't—can't—describe the experience of grief. Since my mother's death, I find myself breaking into sudden sobs. Yet I'm not "sad"—that's not the feeling. Sometimes I'll experience an intense rush of closeness, or of memory, or I'm flooded with passionate love for her.

We're told there are five stages of grief: denial, anger, bargaining, depression, and acceptance. Perhaps that's so—but none of these words describes the actual, very personal, experience—it just describes certain stages. Your anger is different than mine—yours may be felt through shrieks of rage; mine might be a white hot ache.

Your denial might be through dancing and singing; mine might be a catatonic numbness. We may share a process—and, as everyone knows who has experienced death, the process of grief is not linear. It's more like an expanding balloon, those five classic stages layering on top of each other, now this one, now that one, and finally settling around us like a cocoon of acceptance—or at least an acceptance of the inevitability of it all.

Or perhaps when someone we love dies we are thrust inside an enormous cocoon of "grief" (what's the right word?) and slowly those stages are lifted away and we're back to being ourselves again.

How can the brief word "grief" encompass such an experience?

That being said, English is one of the richest languages in the world, blended as it is from many others. Expanding your vocabulary is a tremendous asset to your writing. There is almost always a precise noun for the word you seek to describe using an adjective and a mediocre noun. For example, "windy snow" could be a "blizzard." A "loud shout" could be a "roar." The scrap of food left on your plate could be your "ort."

And some words are unique to certain languages. Here's one:

Mamihlapinatapai is a word from the Yaghan language of Tierra del Fuego and it's almost impossible to translate. Literally it means "one reads in a face many strange matters." But in truth it refers to a look shared by two people, each wishing that the other will offer or say something that they both desire but are unwilling to suggest or offer themselves.

Writing Practice—Play the Game of Dictionary

The Dictionary Game is a word game in which players guess the definition of a word that no one in the group knows. All you need to play this game is a large, unabridged dictionary, and a pencil and pieces of paper for each player.

Each turn consists of one player picking a word from the dictionary and each other player making up a fake definition. Each player gets an opportunity to pick a word.

Here's how to play: The first Picker chooses a word from the dictionary and announces and spells it to the other players. If anyone in the group already knows it, they need to say so and the Picker needs to find a different one.

If a word has more than one definition listed, Pickers can choose which one to use. They can edit the dictionary definition as s/he thinks will fit into the other players' definitions. This is especially important if you're playing with children—make all the definitions sound fairly similar as you're reading them out loud.

Each player writes a definition of the word, initials it, and submits it to the Picker, who shuffles them, including their own correct one. The Picker reads the list out loud—usually trying not to laugh. The Picker may read the definitions in any order. On a second reading, each other player in turn then votes for the definition he or she believes is correct. For obvious reasons, the Picker does not vote. In my rule book, you're not allowed to vote for your own definition—but in some versions of the game this is permitted (it's called 'bluffing.' You don't get points, though, if you choose your own definition.)

Scoring: You earn points if you guess the correct definition of a word and when your made-up definition is selected by another player. If you're the Picker, you get a point if no one votes for your correct definition. You can play around with scoring, though. I've played this game with people who think that if no one guesses the correct definition, the Picker should earn three points.

The best part of this game is how hard it will make you laugh.

I also recommend that you subscribe to Wordsmith.org. This daily word—along with its meaning and etymology—that shows up in your inbox is presented with such lightness, unusualness, and affection that you immediately get a sense that the Anu Garg has a love for words—not just an interest in them. Do you know what a "yob" is and where the word came from?

And what is a lacuna? It's an empty space, gap, missing part, an opening.

Daily Happinesses

lifting the rock and finding a small door
landing on her shoulder
a ream of vellum paper
an antique Spanish chair
knowing the moment is just right for it
laughing your head off
elves hiding under a large mushroom in the rain

August

WEEK 31

Let me love you

A writer never has a vacation. For a writer life consists of either writing or thinking about writing. –Eugene Ionesco

How often have you looked at a sunset and said, "I love that sky!" Or you listened to the radio and said, "I love that song!"

Now is a time to experience this differently. Turn it around.

This is how it happened for me: As I was walking on the beach early one morning, contemplating the years past and the years ahead, filled with intense emotion, relentless thoughts, and focusing on the steady rhythm of my bare feet on cool sand, I heard something—a voice, a feeling? I don't know. But I heard it distinctly. It said: "Listen to the waves." So I stopped and listened for many hours, hearing as though for the first time all the subtleties of the waves, the deep, booming roar of the ocean, the crashes, the whispers, the rustle of the foam on the sand, the sweeping in and the sweeping out of so much water, the endlessness.

The process was like getting to know a strange language I had never heard before. I realized the waves are not individual entities: they speak for the whole ocean. And this is what the waves say, over and over: "I only want to love you. Let me love you."

In that moment the world shifted. I realized that everything in the world longs to love us: the birds, the sky, the wind, the light. Even people! You might think that you enjoy being loved by someone else, but imagine or remember the joy of yourself being in love. And so with nature, or the sand under our feet, or the nose of a puppy. It all wants to love you, as much or more as you love it.

So the next time you look at a sunset, hear it say this to you: "I only want to love you. Let me love you." And when you feel the breeze on your face, or you watch a star twinkle—let it love you. Because that's all it really wants to do.

Love does not alter the beloved, it alters itself. –Soren Kierkegaard

Writing Practice: You Are the Beloved

We've been programmed to think that selflessness and doing good deeds for others are vital for our wellbeing. We've been told that sticking with a lousy job, an abusive boss, and bleak sacrifice is what life is about. Self-denial is part of our existence.

That's all true, to an extent. But it's not the whole story. What matters most in the world is you. You need to care first and foremost about yourself. Everything you do and care and feel and think needs to be with you at your center, no one else. You are the dearest, the kindest human in your life. You are the sun—let the others orbit around you. And that way your light shines on them and they flourish and grow and shine as well.

By loving yourself, I'm not advocating selfishness or greed! It's the opposite, in fact. Greed is *not* loving yourself—greed and selfishness will make you sick, just as it makes the world sick. Loving yourself means being as kind and loving toward yourself as you would be toward someone you love very dearly.

That's all very well and good, I hear you say, but how can we do it? Years of conditioning, of people telling you the opposite or setting your value in terms of wealth or attractiveness or success make it impossible. So what is the process? How can you practice this?

Since you love to write, begin by using Writing as your main practice. How often have you said, "I love that poem!" Or, "What a great word—I love it!" Now turn the experience around: Words, sentences, grammar, stories—they all want to love you. Let them. Let a word adore you.

Allow a sentence to speak its pleasure in being with you. Enjoy the poem's gift of loving you.

Look at a phrase or a paragraph in your story and surrender to it. For this writing practice, the effort is not to feel you are the master of your work. Let it love you. Let it pamper you, take care of you, worship you, adore you. Let the poem say, "This is for *you*. Enjoy!"

Surrender to the love your words have for you.

Think of surrender not as giving up, but giving. Think of it in the same way the sun surrenders to its orbit and the moon surrenders to being a reflection in silver light.

Or the candle surrenders to being lit.

Or a flower surrenders to its own fragrance.

Surrender to being your own light, your own happiness, your own fragrance, your own beating heart. Surrender to yourself.

All else falls into place around you.

You are the beloved.

You must write every single day of your life…You must lurk in libraries and climb the stacks like ladders to sniff books like perfumes and wear books like hats upon your crazy heads….may you be in love every day for the next 20,000 days. And out of that love, remake a world. –Ray Bradbury

Daily Happinesses

precision as you cut the diamond
belonging
a flight of fancy
nestled under the wing of a chicken
merrily parting ways
the road leading back to your door.
what the raven said

WEEK 32

Writing slowly

"Anything worth doing is worth doing slowly." -Mae West

A few years ago I read Carl Honore's *In Praise of Slow,* where he writes about a growing movement that encourages savoring the time you have rather than trying to use it to further another goal—especially in the case of raising our children. He made some powerful points (although he admits he got a speeding ticket while he was researching the book). The Slow Movement has been growing much faster than you might think from its name—and I hope it continues to do so.

Some people (Wikipedia, for example) say the Slow Movement began in 1986, when people protested the opening of a McDonald's restaurant in the beautiful and ancient Piazza di Spagna, Rome. Since then, there have been groups devoted to Slow Food, Slow Parenting, Slow Travel, Slow Design—and most recently I perused Nicole Daedone's exquisitely titled Slow Sex.

Of course the Slow Movement is not all that new: the Romantics and the Transcendentalists propounded living free from the fast-paced, rat-race to nowhere, and instead going inward—to be still and to appreciate being in nature.

The Slow Movement builds on these concepts. There are benefits—ethical, individual, social, and spiritual—to doing what you do at the right speed, that is, the speed that suits the activity. It's bringing mindfulness to your practice. Mindfulness simply means being with what is—no judgment, no analysis: being an active presence in the moment.

If you're not taking pleasure in writing down each word, in savoring the tastes and sounds you describe, in imagining deeply the tenderness or pathos in your character's heart, you're missing out on the most satisfying aspect of writing.

I'm writing a book. I've got the page numbers done. –Stephen Wright

Writing Practice – Slow Writing

Try this for a week or two: let your purpose in doing anything be the activity itself. Even wash your dishes mindfully (skip the dishwasher). Appreciate each lovely dish, let yourself be mesmerized by the sparkling soap bubbles, feel the warm water caressing your fingers, experience the satisfaction of stroking the sink clean.

Put away your laptop for a while and instead get out a pen and a notepad. Now gaze out the window for a while. If possible, wander outside and lie in the hammock.

Write down a word: for example, perhaps that word is 'buttercup.' You want to write for writing's sake. That is the pleasure you get out of doing it.

Buttercup.

Look at the buttercup. Only one buttercup—not all of them. Write down another word. "Sturdy stem." Oops, that's two. Well, that's okay. Feel the breeze on your cheek.

Maybe it's time to eat the chilled raspberries in the refrigerator and describe them. How do they feel on your tongue? Take it slowly—see what words bubble up for you when you're not trying to churn out an article or scene in your novel. You might be surprised at the metaphor that is trying to find its way onto your notepad.

Slow writing is about loving what you're doing and being loved by it. Become intimate with your writing—savor it—treat it like a lover. You'll be amazed how it reciprocates.

I learned that you should feel when writing, not like Lord Byron on a mountain top, but like a child stringing beads in kindergarten,happy, absorbed and quietly putting one bead on after another. –Brenda Ueland

Daily Happinesses

going to the movies in the afternoon
dressing up
cantering on a black horse across the moor
spending a rainy afternoon exploring the attics
just before waking up
hundreds of redwings in the field
a lightning storm on the far side of the bay

WEEK 33

Message in a bottle

Life is a little like a message in a bottle, to be carried by the winds and the tides. –Gene Tierney

What an extraordinary invention bottles are.

There are green glass bottles. Tiny cobalt blue bottles. Clear bottles. Short squat amber ones that you'd find in an apothecary. Hand blown bottles from Venice. Chianti bottles from Italy. Stainless steel bottles. Exquisite perfume bottles. Round, thin, long-necked, wide-bottomed… bottles come in just about every shape, color, size imaginable. And their purposes are inexhaustible.

Almost like people.

Do you remember the first time you saw a ship in a bottle? Wasn't that the most wonderful, impossible vision, when you didn't have a clue how the ship got inside?

How often have you wondered how a genie exists in a bottle? What kind of place does a being who can grant you three wishes create for itself? Is it fiery and steamy inside, or murky, or filled with opulence and fragrance?

The world is full of genies waiting to grant your wishes. -Percy Ross

Writing Practice – Messages

Imagine this: You are on a lush island, sitting under a palm tree on a silk-sand beach. You have seven small pieces of paper and a pencil. You also have seven small bottles with sturdy corks in each.

Every morning, for seven days, write a brief message that would be inserted into one of the bottles and tossed into the ocean. What would you write down, if you wanted to communicate the most important thing in the world at that moment? Imagine that your message would be retrieved by a stranger on a shore in a far-off land.

Sometimes our conversations, and writings, and even are thoughts, are just too noisy. Pare down the excess, stop trying to communicate too much, take a deep breath and go slow. Take it easy.

If there was only one thing to say, and it was to a stranger, what would it be?

Whenever you have truth it must be given with love, or the message and the messenger will be rejected. –Mahatma Gandhi

Daily Happinesses

greeted with a bouquet of flowers from the garden
pelicans and herons asleep in the mangroves
seeing yourself as a child
rain drops on black boughs and twigs
flying east, into the dawn
a circular slant of light
finding yourself transported back in time

WEEK 34

Napping makes you smarter

Think what a better world it would be if we all, the whole world, had cookies and milk about three o'clock every afternoon and then lay down on our blankets for a nap. –Robert Fulghum

A study by Harvard University researchers claims that taking a nap makes you smarter!

It's been known for a while that a good night's sleep makes you think and act more clearly and quickly. While you sleep, anything that you've just learned—including information for tests or a new skill—gets integrated in your brain. Napping for an hour or two has a similar benefit. Combining a night's sleep with an afternoon nap has twice the effect on your brain that only a night's sleep does. In other words, "Divided sleep is more recuperative than sleep taken in a single block," says Gregory Belenky, who's a Research Professor and Director of the Sleep and Performance Research Center at Washington State University.

There are lots of statistics you can research for yourselves to find out more about the wonderful topic of napping, including NASA's findings that pilots who nap (not while on the job but in between, we hope) increase their alertness and performance by as much as 50%.

I've always felt that most people undervalue the beauty and importance of sleep. Napping has a stigma of laziness attached to it—except in those wise Mediterranean, Latin, and South Pacific countries where it's taken for granted. This stigma is especially hard on teenagers, who are deluged with constantly new information, new experiences, and new social situations that have to be dealt with, and are required to wake up much too early, and told not to put their heads down on their desk after lunch ... think how much smarter a whole rising generation would be if they were assigned nap periods as part of their daily schedule!

For many people, napping is also deeply enjoyable. Do you feel entitled and happy when you enjoy a nice leisurely walk or watch a movie ... but you regard taking a nap as indolent? Time to change that way of thinking. Not only is napping beneficial to your physical and mental well-being, but it's highly pleasurable as well, and pleasure is a good thing.

I usually take a two hour nap from one to four. -Yogi Berra

Writing Practice – Take a nap

Here's your task: Spend several hours on your WIP, have a tasty light lunch, and then take a nap for an hour or an hour-and-a-half.

Ideally, do this around two o'clock, when your body's clock dips way down in energy and alertness. You'll join the ranks of Napoleon Bonaparte, Winston Churchill, and John F. Kennedy, who all took naps during some of the most crucial moments in history.

I catnap now and then, but I think while I nap,
so it's not a waste of time." -Martha Stewart

Daily Happinesses

the Holy Feet of the Sri Gomatheswar statue, Sravanabelagola
biting into a just-picked apple
Meteora, Greece, at dawn
being unexpectedly kissed
the sweetest crescent moon
papaya salad
stepping onto the gangplank

September

Week 35 — A place of your own
Week 36 — Castling, forking, and making luft
Week 37 – Ask yourself: "Is this vital?"
Week 38 — Show, don't tell
Week 39 — Surprise!

WEEK 35

A Place of Your Own

Some places speak distinctly. Certain dank gardens cry aloud for a murder; certain old houses demand to be haunted; certain coasts are set apart for shipwrecks. –Robert Louis Stevenson

As I was conversing with a WriteSpa client, and we were discussing assignments and goals, I asked her where she wrote. She hesitated, then said, "It's a bit problematic… I don't have a laptop and my computer's in the living room. I don't really have a place for it."

From the way she spoke, I could tell that using "the computer" was for her a chore, a bit of a nuisance, something that she 'should' turn on and use, like a vacuum cleaner. I knew that for her to have a satisfying relationship with "Mr. (or Ms.) Write," the ambience surrounding the area where she worked was crucial.

This is not true for everyone. I have friends who are most inspired to write when they're with a crowd of strangers at a Starbucks. Harriet Beecher Stowe wrote on the dining room table, in the midst of a great deal of hustle and bustle. Jane Austen snuck her time in between morning calls (which happen, by the way, in the afternoon). Some authors write in their head, some in bed, some can only do it with a secretary on hand to take down the words.

You need to know what works for you in terms of place. You need to decide what makes you feel secure, at ease, and in a space that you can enjoy. Even if you have to squeeze in Writing between a cup of coffee and taking the kids to school, you'll find much more pleasure if you surround that brief time with ritual, with some form of beauty, with its own mood.

What is needed is, in the end, simply this: solitude, great inner solitude. Going into yourself and meeting no one for hours on end-- that is what you must be able to attain. –Rainer Maria Rilke

Writing Practice – Setting Up Your Space

Fragrance: No matter where you choose to write, decide on a fragrance that you will use exclusively for writing. Choose an essential oil that speaks to you—sandalwood, rosewood, jasmine . . . whatever you'd like, but one that is not too familiar. Save it for Writing. Smell this each time you're preparing to open your document. You'll find it helps enormously when, in the weeks and months to come, you find yourself stuck, depressed, or distracted from Writing, or if you find yourself traveling in another town, far from home, and yearn to write. Through your olfactory glands, your habit of finding pleasure in Writing will be triggered in your memory, and will be reignited. Create the habit now.

Do something that is beautiful for your writing space. Place a vase of flowers nearby, for example. Or a crystal. A piece of colored silk. A pinecone. Something that harmonizes and centers you, and reminds you that this moment is between you and Flow and nothing else. If you're planning on taking your laptop to the local coffee shop, wear a color that inspires, or slip on a pair of soft socks or charming shoes you particularly like.

Personally speaking, I wouldn't listen to music while I write. I know music inspires many people, but I think it undermines the relationship between your heart and your words, because your heart is pulled by the music on the machine, instead of the music of the spheres. Try writing without artificial music for a while and see what happens. You can always go back to it.

I think that comfort is essential. A supporting chair, or soft couch, or a bed piled high with luxurious pillows—

choose what makes you comfortable, but *be comfortable*. This exercise is about loving the experience of Writing. It's about appreciating its worth in your life—not about angst, feeling scratchy, or suffering. It's about wonder, awe, gratitude—and opening another window into what it means to be human.

The ideal view for daily writing, hour for hour, is the blank brick wall of a cold-storage warehouse. Failing this, a stretch of sky will do, cloudless if possible. –Edna Ferber

Daily Happinesses

the loud sound of a leaf falling on a still afternoon
a silver fish in a silver net that can talk and grant wishes
swimming in a mountain lake in autumn
a small favor that resonates
scraping off the barnacles
arriving at the temple of Banteay Srei in Cambodia
the grapes ripening

WEEK 36

The greatest rules of dramatic writing are conflict, conflict, conflict. –James Frey

Castling, forking, and making luft

I loathe conflict, which, for a novelist, is a terrible thing. This summer I tried to appreciate conflict by playing chess, after many years' hiatus.

Here's how Manly Hall describes the game of chess (The Secret Teachings of All Ages, chapter XXIV): "The chessboard consists of 64 squares alternately black and white and symbolizes the floor of the House of the Mysteries. Upon this field of existence or thought move a number of strangely carved figures, each according to fixed law. The white king is Ormuzd; the black king, Ahriman; and upon the plains of Cosmos the great war between Light and Darkness is fought through all the ages. Of the philosophical constitution of man, the kings represent the spirit; the queens the mind; the bishops the emotions; the knights the vitality; the castles, or rooks, the physical body. The pieces upon the kings' side are positive; those upon the queens' side, negative. The pawns are the sensory impulses and perceptive faculties—the eight parts of the soul... The game of chess sets forth the eternal struggle of each part of man's compound nature against the shadow of itself. The nature of each of the chessmen is revealed by the way in which it moves; geometry is the key to their interpretation. The castle (the body) moves on the square; the bishop (the emotions) moves on the slant; the king, being the spirit, cannot be captured, but loses the battle when so surrounded that it cannot escape."

From the time I was eight till around sixteen years old, my father and I used to play chess practically every night. I became absorbed not just in the strategy, but in the characteristics of the pieces. Pawns were brave but not very skilled. Bishops were clever. Knights were maverick and tricky—rather like guerilla fighters. Rooks were strong and powerful, but they needed a lot of room to maneuver. And don't get me started on the talented, adept, versatile queen who gracefully defended the kingdom for her dull, quiet, fuddy-duddy old king.

Stories can be written about anything in the world—and character given to just about anything as well. A plump teapot, a sheer, terrifying cliff, a roiling sky... Even typefaces have distinct personalities. But chess pieces are the best things in the world to characterize. When I played chess, wondering what each piece was thinking and feeling was far more vivid to me than the action.

Still, one of the most important qualities I learned from those evenings was the importance of learning to finish. Even when it was obvious I was going to lose, my father would turn the chess board around and say: "Practice your end game." We both knew I was strongest in the opening—where I could be impulsive, brave, and safely move quickly. But when it came time to actually close in on that poor old king, I tended to tune out. Not any longer. After so many years of finishing a game, it makes me slightly ill to have to interrupt one—or leave any story unfinished.

My re-emergence into the world of chess inspired me to take up another old favorite: Sun Tzu's *Art of War*. He has some excellent advice (replace 'war' with 'story-telling').

"In the practical art of war, the best thing of all is to take the enemy's country whole and intact; to shatter and destroy it is not good. So, too, it is better to recapture an entire army than to destroy it, to capture a regiment, a detachment or a company entire than to destroy them." In other words, if you're trying to win your lady or get the job, you don't do it by storming her apartment or surrounding that office. Getting to the heart of the matter from within works much better—and creates a much better novel.

And Sun Tzu describes six types of terrain, one of which he calls Precipitous Heights. "If you are beforehand with your adversary, you should occupy the raised and sunny spots and from there wait for him to come up." In other words...arrange a picnic.

The truth is that our finest moments are most likely to occur when we are feeling deeply uncomfortable, unhappy, or unfulfilled. For it is only in such moments, propelled by our discomfort, that we are likely to step out of our ruts and start searching for different ways or truer answers. –M. Scott Peck

Writing Practice – Make Luft, Not War

Select a chess piece (or two) and write a short story using that piece as the protagonist.

Narrate your story from a first-person point of view, building on the idiosyncrasies of the personality of the chess piece. Write it in a dreamy, fairy-tale style. Describe the town and the fields and the woods around, as well as the battle itself. Remember to stay in character: a rook is not going to sneak up on a pawn early in the game, although it might come up behind you near the end.

Did you know that "Romantic chess" was the style of chess prevalent in the 19th century, and characterized by bold attacks and sacrifices.

Intersperse lots of melodrama and emotion into your story. You might even want to write something like "Ah, me!" when the queen is dragged off in chains to the enemy dungeon. Perhaps you are a pawn, and your only goal is to reach the opponent's side to rescue her. Will you make it?

Write at least three paragraphs: beginning, middle, and end. Here is your title, your characters, and some plot devices you can use:

Title: Alekhine's Gun (this is a formation in which a queen backs up two rooks).

Characters:

Caïssa (she's the goddess of chess, invoked for good luck: "Caïssa was with me").

A man (a piece or a pawn. Note that the queen is also a man). (This makes it interesting.)

The bad bishop or, if you prefer, the wrong-colored bishop.

A duffer, or fish, is a weak player. You could also call him a patzer or woodpusher.

Things that can happen:

Kick: This is when a pawn attacks a piece, forcing it to move.

Offer a gambit—a sacrifice.

Go for a normal fork.

Or enjoy a family fork, or a family check.

Passer is a pawn who's passed. (Not necessarily passed on or passed over. Just passed.)

Hanging pawns are two friendly pawns without friendly pawns on either side. Pawns are brilliant. You can write about poisoned pawn and pawn storms.

Trébuchet—I thought this was a font! But actually it's a position of mutual zugzwang in which either player would lose if it is their turn to move.

You can always invoke the J'adoube—in which you adjust things without being subject to the touched piece rule. Like unbuttoning the top button, but not feeling around further…

I like this one best: make luft (by making space for a castled king to prevent a back rank mate.)

But make sure you use the prophylaxis, a move that frustrates an opponent's plan or tactic.

And don't leave out the "Mysterious rook move." No one knows what this is.

Another option—if you don't feel like writing today—is to play chess or re-read *The Art of War*. You'll be inspired.

Conflict is the gadfly of thought. It stirs us to observation and memory. It instigates to invention. It shocks us out of sheeplike passivity, and sets us at noting and contriving. –John Dewey

Daily Happinesses

browsing in second-hand bookstores
a spider web covered with dew
filled with sweet, ripe blackberries
heavy velvet curtains
knowing it's time
a series of unexpected events that leads to amazement
curled up on a window-seat with a mystery

WEEK 37

My importance to the world is relatively small. One other hand, my importance to myself is tremendous. I am all I have to work with, to play with, to suffer, and to enjoy. –Noel Coward

Ask yourself: "Is this vital?"

When I worked at the last stressful job I hope I'll ever have, a sensitive and intelligent board member pointed out the reason I was having such a hard time: "Since you're constantly trying to fend off the alligators, you have no time to drain the swamp."

Take a look at your day. Most of us are fending off alligators all day long: whether it's because we're working at a job that is understaffed, or we're overwhelmed taking care of young children, or we're running a company, or we're simply trying to pay the bills.

How do we drain the swamp, and drive those alligators away?

Before my board member friend spoke to me, I had organized everything into three folders:

- Urgent
- Important
- Must-do

Makes sense, right? But because of the nature of my work, I was always reaching for my Urgent—or "alligator"—folder. I couldn't miss a press release or advertising deadline! I had to make that call before such-and-such a date! And so forth. Because the Urgent folder filled up on a daily—or even hourly—basis, I rarely touched the Important—or "swamp"—folder. And the Must-do file was ignored and became quite plump.

It wasn't until I swapped the labels on "Urgent" and "Important" that I finally got my head above water. For one hour every day, I pretended I was at a crucial meeting. I refused phone calls, locked my office door, and began to plow through what had been just the "Important" folder but now became "Urgent." Once these longer-term items were addressed, the alligators began to diminish. I found I wasn't going to drown and be eaten up after all.

Maybe your current Urgent folder is not a stressful office job but a houseful of babies (or even just one!). Can you swap your thinking around taking care of your baby? Your baby is Important—but she's not (or at least rarely) Urgent. (What may be Urgent is for you to attend a yoga class, or take a night out with a friend. Or ask your mom or a friend to take your baby to the park, so you can have the house to yourself for one hour. And for heaven's sake, don't wash the dishes or run around picking up socks during that hour! That's Must-Do, not Urgent! Urgent means: Have a long, aromatic bath. Read a book. Write in your diary. Make love. Be alone. Be with your spouse.)

I no longer have babies to keep me from writing, and I left the stress of a job I didn't love a long time ago. But prioritizing is still a challenge: Urgent tasks such as communicating with clients and friends, organizing freelance work, meeting my own deadlines, invoicing, and generally clearing the decks tend to take precedence over the most vital work which, for me, is Writing.

We could spend hours on these seemingly urgent things. Yes, the dishes need to be washed. Yes, a client needs a call back. And maybe we're one of those people who has a problem focusing unless everything is "just right." But creativity is not going to flow unless we place it in our Urgent folder, and deal with everything else as just Important.

The key is not to prioritize what's on your schedule,
but to schedule your priorities. –Stephen Covey

Writing Practice – "Is this Vital?"

Imagine that your creative work is the only thing in your Urgent folder: it is what you need to get to before anything else is attended to. If you have a job or children or other obligations that are going to impede on the time you've set yourself for creative work, ask yourself: "Is this task vital?" Using that word will help you put your priorities into perspective. Is it vital that the floor is mopped? Is it vital that you open that email?

Only something vital should impede your creative time.

This week, make writing—or any creative endeavor—a priority. Your creative body is just that: a body that needs to be treated with as much care and respect as a boss, an employee, a friend, a baby. If you consistently put that body aside in favor of other, more pressing, items that require your attention, you may wake up one day and find that it's not sitting around waiting for you. Your creative life is not something to take for granted.

Begin with a routine that heralds the space and time that writing requires. Turn off all the distractions that make it so hard to be in that creative space—your phone especially. Light a candle, or make that coffee or green tea, or ring a sacred bell, or play a short melody on your recorder. Do something significant that says "Now I begin." In that space and time, even if you spend it only looking out of the window or staring at your screen, you're allowing your creative body to enter. Love it as you would a baby or a lover! Love that space and time—and let it be. You'll establish a habit that automatically ensures Creativity will be there for you, because you have shown that you are there for it.

The hardest part about prioritizing in this way is that you're challenging typical expectations. You may find your friends, colleagues, clients, and relatives expect you to place them in the Urgent folder and are deeply hurt that you shut them out. From the time we were young children, we've been told that artistic creative "fun" play is not nearly as urgent as learning the alphabet and the times tables, much less a visit from Great Aunt Augusta or a call from your boss. Question that! Fly in the face of the mindset of the world around you. Your inner voice, your creative soul, your longing to write is the most vital thing in the world! Be available to it.

Because in the end are you going to remember a deadline you missed or the time you didn't wash the dishes? Or are you going remember the peace and satisfaction of writing a poem or rereading a story that poured out of you one morning, early?

You... will not always be able to solve all of the world's problems at once but don't ever underestimate the importance you can have... courage can be contagious and hope can take on a life of its own. –Michelle Obama

Daily Happinesses

the path through the woods at dusk
a pelican on the beach in Mykonos
being handed a long-stemmed rose
a box at the opera
four quartz crystals in a pool of water
opening the drawer and finding a mysterious charm bracelet
the shepherd home from the hill

WEEK 38

Caress the detail, the divine detail. –Vladimir Nabokov

Show, don't tell

One of the hardest things to do is to write in a way that is not so much visual as it is moody. A lake can be ominous or serene with the lightest of adjectives. A look can be like a dagger or a rose—but it's the same eyes, the same face, the same person. What makes it different? It's how it's described.

The most well-known adage in writing classes is "show, don't tell." Don't say, "The night was dark"—describe it. Was it still and serene and an enchanted fairy ring is about to emerge in your story? Or are ominous clouds obliterating the stars, one by one? Is there sound—a horseman riding by, or the strange noise of the city at night? One of my favorite writing exercises when I'm teaching is to get students to describe a 'dark and stormy night' without mentioning dark, stormy, or night. Show it. Describe the thick clouds that obscure the moon, or evoke a sense of the sultry heat that feels like a suffocating blanket. What you're trying to convey is why it's dark. Fear? Tension? Grief? An alchemical insight about to occur? Is it the darkest hour of life? Or is dawn about to pale the sky?

Here is what happens when you "tell" a story. "I sat down at the table, picked up a knife and fork, and began to eat. Mary did too. We didn't say anything."

Here is what happens you "show" the same story: "I sat on the hard chair, my throat closing up at the smell of egg. The knife glinted metallic as I stared at it. Then I looked up and met Mary's hostile eyes. I picked up the fork, determined not to speak first. The sound of cutlery on our plates clattered in the silence."

Part of the effect comes from detail. Paying attention to detail is crucial to storytelling. Are the curtains yellow or mustard? Is the car red or black?

Another way to enrich the "showing" is using senses other than sight. Is the fragrance in the air fishy or ocean-fresh? Are you tasting fear? Is the sound of a hammer banging in the background angry or constructive? Don't tell us that the house looks lonely in the middle of that field. Show us that it's barricaded by tall ornamental grasses, and the tinted windows reflect the setting sun, ensuring privacy, and the swimming pool is always immaculately clean—and never used.

If you're taking to heart these important aspects I've mentioned of evoking a mood by observing detail and using all five senses, and you won't use meaningless words or phrases like "she was beautiful" or "it was amazing" or "incredible" or "handsome." Be specific, be inventive, and enjoy the wealth of words and images that come when you're really showing us what's going on inside.

The business of the novelist is not to relate great events,
but to make small ones interesting. – Arthur Schopenhauer

Writing Practice: Rainy evenings and climbing trees

John Gardner, in *On Writing Fiction* (highly recommended!), offers an excellent writing practice: to describe an old barn from the point of a view of a young woman who's just gotten (happily) married and an old man whose son was just killed in the war. The caveat: don't mention barn, or young woman, or old man, or death, or marriage. Just describe the barn.

Here are seven exercises for you to do this week that will deepen and enrich your skill in showing, not telling. Try one every day and it'll become a natural part of your writing. I believe that even the most talented and experienced writers need to do these on a regular basis. It's like practicing scales if you're a pianist. Careful, detailed, neutral observation is at the foundation of all inspired writing.

Each exercise requires two paragraphs. Use the same setting and the same time of day for both paragraphs, but describe them differently. A full moon can be romantic or it can be crazy-making and desperate. Stars can be cold and indifferent or low and friendly. The peeling paint can be a sign of decay or of a long, cozy history in the house.

1. ***A rainy evening.*** Describe a rainy evening from the point of view of a young man who's considering suicide. Don't mention rain, evening, young man, or suicide. Create a mood of loneliness, despair, and hopelessness. You can describe a stuffy, overheated living room, for example, with an oppressive aunt seated by the fire, and thick curtains drawn, blocking out any lingering light. Or you can describe the soaking wet forest and the sound of the torrential river in the distance. Now describe the same rainy evening (again without mentioning rain or evening)

and but from the point of view of a young man who has fallen in love and is waiting for his beloved to arrive. If you described the first paragraph as you walked through the woods, use the exact same scene, just describe it differently. The forest won't be soaking wet—it will be sparkling and fresh. The earth will smell moist—the river is not frightening but inviting.

2. ***Getting on the boat.*** Describe this experience from the point of view of a child who's leaving his home—and everything he knows and loves—behind. Then describe the same experience of getting on a boat from the point of view of a wrongly-accused man who's being deported but plans to escape to freedom and a new life. Don't mention child or home, wrongly-accused man, deportation, freedom, or new life. Just describe how it feels to be getting on the boat. What do you smell? Salt—like a wound? Or salt—like flavor and excitement? Is the sky blue with grief or blue with hope? Are the windswept clouds parting and disintegrating or closing in on the ship and presaging a storm?

3. ***The wedding gown.*** Describe a wedding gown from the point of view of a woman who's being forced into an unpleasant marriage and then from the point of view of a woman who's madly in love with the groom-to-be. Just tell us about the dress—no background.

4. ***A thrilling sports play*** from the point of view of a fan of the winning team and then fan of the losing team. Don't mention fan—just describe the action.

5. ***A still mountain lake*** from the point of view of a woman who is pregnant and delighted with the upcoming birth. The same lake, same time of day, seen from the point of view of someone who has just committed a murder.

6. ***Consulting the oracle:*** Describe a gypsy fortune teller who is honest, authentic, wise, kind and positively encouraging. (Don't use any of those words). Then describe her or him again, but know that he or she is a charlatan, a cheat, a user, and even frightening. Don't use any of those words either—convey the personality through the clothes, the surroundings, smells, sounds, and perhaps even the taste of the tea you drink…

7. ***Climbing a tree:*** You're climbing a tree to escape and hide from something terrifying. You're climbing the same tree for pleasure and to find a lovely place to daydream. Don't tell us what you're running away from or what you're daydreaming about. Just describe the tree, the branches, the blossoms, the breeze—remember to include all your senses in the experience to place your reader at the heart of the action.

There are three rules for writing the novel. Unfortunately, no one knows what they are. –Somerset Maugham

Daily Happinesses

Fire sparks from a bonfire floating to the stars
a small cafe in the south of France
sleeping soundly throughout the night
meeting at the street fair
setting down the pen with a deep sigh of relief
an island of good luck
tending to your baby llama

WEEK 39

Surprise is the greatest gift which life can grant us. –Boris Pasternak

Surprise!

Twists and surprises are my favorite aspects of stories. I love them. My favorite page-turning novels are not violent, terrifying, deep, or beautiful. They are surprising. And if you love something, do it. My advice to writers: write what you love to read.

Recently I re-read *Rebecca* and, even though I feel I know it by heart, three scenes still create a frisson of pleasurable shock when I read them: Mr. de Winter's totally unexpected, appalled reaction when the nameless heroine descends the staircase for the ball; Mr. de Winter's astounding declaration that he hated his former wife; and the final revelation in the doctor's office…

In *Jane Eyre* the twist arrives just at the point when we believe she's going to be married and live happily ever after. What on earth could go wrong now? Uh oh… a secret revealed. The book goes off on another tangent—one that is entirely unexpected.

There are hundreds of examples. The master of plot twists is still, in my opinion, Alfred Hitchcock. Watch *North by Northwest* again, and analyze the unexpected surprises that occur in every single scene. You have no idea what will reveal itself next.

Hitchcock once described the difference between suspense and surprise in this way (I'm paraphrasing):

Suspense: A man walks along the street, carrying a briefcase. In the briefcase is a bomb. We know the bomb is there, and we know he has to get it from point A to point B, or else …

Surprise: A man walks along the street, carrying a briefcase. We do not know what is in the briefcase, or where he is going. Suddenly the bomb explodes and the man is killed.

I think one of the things Hitchcock means by this example is that if we as readers or viewers are placed in the mind and heart of the protagonist, we are more breathless and engaged than if we don't know what's going on. In other words, don't tease your readers by keeping them out of the loop of what you, as a writer, know. Partner with your readers: make them feel you're in this adventure together.

Suspense does not have to be gruesome or violent. A good page-turner, though, needs several good story surprises during its unfolding. It needs occurrences that are fresh and bright, and that you did not see coming.

So, how do you create twists and surprises in your story? Here are seven traditional methods:

Anagnorisis: From the Greek word meaning 'recognition,' anagnorisis describes a plot twist or surprise that has to do with a revelation or discovery. The most familiar occurs in Sophocles's play *Oedipus Rex,* when a messenger reveals to Oedipus his true birth, and he learns that the fate he would much rather have avoided ("you will kill your father and marry your mother") has indeed come to pass in spite of everything he did to prevent it. As far as we know, Aristotle first coined the word and describes several different kinds of anagnorisis—the most common being when someone recognizes a birthmark or a familiar locket.

Assumption: Breaking down assumptions is your greatest gift you can offer as storytellers. I'll never forget the first time I heard this puzzle: "A man on his way to work first drives his son to school. On the way there, he is in a car accident and is killed. The boy is badly injured and is taken to the hospital. The doctor is urgently summoned to operate, walks into the hospital room, stops short, and exclaims, "I can't operate on that boy. He's my son!" Most of you nowadays will have no difficulty solving this puzzle, but that wasn't always the case! Surprise your reader in your story by breaking down assumptions. For example, the ghost story turns out to have been told by the ghost. Or, time is not a concept but a real person. Try to imagine something inside out or upside down.

Chekhov's Gun: As any good set designer knows, you don't place a prop on the stage that isn't relevant to the play. Everything has to matter. The concept of Chekhov's Gun is named after playwright Anton Chekhov, who wrote: "If in the first act you have hung a pistol on the wall, then in the following one it should be fired. Otherwise don't put it there." Used in novels, this is also called foreshadowing, and what makes the device particularly interesting is when the foreshadowing turns into something unexpected.

Deus Ex Machina: If you've written your way into a seemingly unsolvable plot, you can always throw in a random fated event to extricate yourself. From the Latin "god as fate" (literally, "god out of the machine"), deus ex machina describes a twist or plot device that occurs not just unexpectedly but also unbelievably. In other words, the author has not paved the way for this intervention. For example, in ancient Greek plays, a god might be lowered to the stage on a crane to randomly solve the problem. This is a story-teller's easiest way to solve a complicated plot. It can be a lot of fun, and a good way to bring humor into a story.

In Medias Res: Beginning a story with this convention ensures that you snap your reader right into a surprise. In Latin, in medias res means "in the middle of something." You start with the action, or a tense moment, and offer no backdrop or back story. Afterward, each scene unfolds as a complete surprise, because the back story is revealed in tandem with the action itself. You can even start with the end—as in the fabulous opening scene of *Sunset Boulevard.*

MacGuffin: a plot element that drives the plot since everyone in the story will do anything to chase it or go after it, even if they hardly know what it is. A macguffin may be ultimately completely unimportant to the plot and sometimes even unexplained. It's not like a red herring, because it's not a device used to distract the reader from the main clues—it's more of a thrusting forward that is eventually forgotten by the end of the film. Alfred Hitchcock's *The 39 Steps* is a classic example: the secret papers being smuggled out of the country have very little to do with the actual plot. In Mel Brooks's comic movie *High Anxiety* a mysterious phone call from "Mr. MacGuffin" (ha) takes us on a different turn. Use a macguffin to drive your story in an unexpected direction: this device helps you think outside the box and frees you from sinking into clichés.

Red herring: The opposite of Chekhov's gun, a red herring is something that distracts the reader from the real clues, and surprises the reader or viewer when the actual truth is revealed. It's important when you use a red herring in your writing that you don't make the reader feel tricked though. Don't overdo.

That element of surprise is what I look for when I am writing. It is my way of judging what I am doing – which is never an easy thing to do. –V. S. Naipaul

Writing Practice – How to Write Surprisingly

Here's something fun:

Invite one or two (or three or four or more) friends over and play a favorite game of all times: Exquisite Corpse.

First played by the Surrealists, this 'game' is based on a much earlier English parlor game called Consequences (which is how I used to play it as a young girl in England.) Someone starts a story by writing a few sentences (you decide on the rules) and folds the piece of paper over so that only the end of the sentence is visible. The next person takes the paper and continues the story, and then hands it to the next person.

As children, we are more familiar with the picture-drawing version of the game, which is why the Surrealists called it Exquisite Corpse. One person draws the feet, leaving the lines leading into the shins for the next person to draw the legs. Remember the astonishment and laughter that emerged when the paper was finally unfolded to reveal a whole human being that surprised us all!

Begin each round by choosing one of these plot devices I described (anagnorisis, assumptions, Chekhov's gun, deus ex machina, in medias res, macguffin, red herring) and agree to grow your story around it. Agree on a title, and perhaps the name of a protagonist, but leave the rest open.

Make sure you agree—just as when you're drawing a picture—that each person knows which part of the story they're going to write. If you want to, follow the five-act outline of Shakespeare, Hollywood films, and Robert McGee:

- Set-up
- Action
- Plot twist
- Climax
- Denouement

If your group is small—two or three of you—you can pass the story around more than once. And don't get stuck with too many rules. For example, if you're using the five-act outline, break it up or go around the circle more than once. Make up your own way of playing this game.

The reason this game is inspiring is that it takes you outside your own assumption about how the story should unfold. Someone else is thinking something completely differently, and as the story moves hither and thither, you become increasingly flexible as a writer and a storyteller. For example, trust is betrayed just when you thought a new character should enter the room. Or a lie is revealed just as you were imagining a passionate embrace was going to occur. Disaster strikes instead of a character's true motive being revealed—or vice versa.

Have fun.

A story to me means a plot where there is some surprise. Because that is how life is—full of surprises. –Isaac Bashevis Singer

Daily Happinesses

climbing the monkeypod tree
discovering a mineral that's never been seen before
lighting the torches before you set off
colorful ribbons and trim for sewing
reflections in a train window
the foundation as deep as the steeple is high
partying with treefrogs all night long

WINSLOW ELIOT
WriteSpa
Writing through the year . . .

October

WEEK 40

A teacher affects eternity: he can never tell where his influence stops. -Henry Adams

Be your own teacher

In 1963, when I was seven years old, my parents took me on a freighter trip around the world "to teach me geography." When we finally landed back in New York City, I was put into a second grade classroom taught by Mrs. Zay. I had never been to school before, and Mrs. Zay appeared to me like an extraordinary Goddess of Children. Her classroom glowed with beauty—it was naturally and simply decorated with rocks, crystals, flowers, and leaves. She was an artist, and her blackboard drawings came alive with shining colors. Everything she did, whether it was the words she chose to speak with, her round, clear writing on the blackboard, or the way she kindly instructed a student to sweep the floor or water the plants—was with complete attention and love.

She taught by example.

I was only in her class for half a year because we went a-traveling again, but because of my parents' unorthodox lifestyle, we'd return to New York at least once a year throughout my childhood, and I'd be plopped back into Mrs. Zay's classroom. The methodology of the Waldorf school is such that one 'main' teacher remains with the class from 1st through 8th grades, so Mrs. Zay became a lodestone in my early years. When I was abroad, I wrote long letters to her, sent her postcards and gifts from far-off places. And whenever I was back in the States, I knew she'd always be there for me.

I grew up and we lost touch. Then, when my own daughter was in second grade, I encountered Mrs. Zay again—teaching second grade at an entirely different school in a different state! I didn't know how I'd move so that my daughter could have her as a teacher, but I'll never forget Mrs. Zay saying with the quiet, kind authority I remembered well: "If your daughter needs to be here, you will make it happen."

And it was true: I found work and a place to live, and Mrs. Zay was my daughter's beloved teacher for the next several years. In one of her earliest essays she describes a beautiful 'garden of children' that Mrs. Zay grows.

These are some of the things her students remember: the feeling of reverence she had for everything. Never wasting anything—it was a point of pride for us to draw with our beeswax crayons until there was hardly anything left. Always singing while we did our chores. Taking out the compost for fun. Playing recorder every morning. Long walks in nature while she told us compelling stories about people like St. Francis and Zarathustra.

Semi-retired now, Jean Zay is the librarian in my daughter's former school, and I try as often as possible to visit her sunny, peaceful room, simply to be in her presence. Even after all these years, she continues to inspire me with her grace, kindness, and beauty, and, most of all, her quality of "always being there" for me.

One looks back with appreciation to the brilliant teachers, but with gratitude to those who touched our human feelings. The curriculum is so much necessary raw material, but warmth is the vital element for the growing plant and for the soul of the child. -Carl Jung

Writing Practice – Imagine Being Your Own Teacher

We all need teachers. Sometimes they come in the guise of mentors, sometimes as friends, sometimes your children can be your teachers. Teaching and learning is the essence of living.

Imagine yourself as a child—your sense of wonder is still vibrant, and your eager soul and open heart shine from you. Now imagine a guide approaches and states: "I am your teacher."

Can you describe this being? What language is spoken, which words are used? Is the lesson filled with play, with games, with depth, with wisdom, with drawing and color? With music?

When you were a child, what kind of class did you long to be a part of?

My grandmother, Ethel Cook Eliot, wrote a children's book called *The Wind Boy,* in which a young girl, Gentian, who struggles in school, finds herself in a classroom in The Clear Land, where she understands easily what the loving, patient teacher instructs her in, where play and camaraderie is an essential part of the learning process, and, best of all, she finds a friend.

I was homeschooled in my early years, and I loved playing on my rocky beach on a Greek island, but when I walked into Mrs. Zay's serene classroom in New York City for the first time, and saw the flower-like rows of boys and girls all staring at me, I thought I was in the most magical place in the world. What would your ideal be? Perhaps you just want to curl up in a window-seat and read all day—your books are your teacher. Perhaps you long to follow a stream—and the stream is your teacher.

Imagine you are your own best teacher.

Because you are!

You are your own best teacher, so you may as well learn to learn from yourself. To trust yourself and enjoy the daily classes! To approach yourself with the wonder and passion of your child-nature. In this writing practice, visualize precisely the teacher you wish you had, and then become that being.

It's never too late to go to school.

It is the supreme art of the teacher to awaken joy in creative expression and knowledge. –Albert Einstein

Daily Happinesses

toast, olive oil, fresh tomatoes, and garlic
the astonishing world of honeybees
new pajamas
a gift card
the smell of fresh ground coffee wafting onto the street
knowing the emptiness
diving in

WEEK 41

"Life is pleasant. Death is peaceful.
It's the transition that's troublesome." –Isaac Azimov

Transitions

I wonder whether we pay enough attention to the delicate time of transitioning from one thing to the next. Moving from playtime to bedtime can bring on a tantrum. Moving from one job to another may not bring on a tantrum, but it can be devastating. Moving from an old home to a new one can be soul-shattering. Transitioning from one season to the next can bring on depression, anxiety, exhaustion.

In school, transitions between classes are some of the most challenging. The end of a class is typically marked by the loud clang of a bell and a frantic rush to finish. Students jump to their feet, their spirits jabbed by shards of noise and movement.

Becoming aware of transitions can help us all through our daily lives. Every single thing we do needs a moment of transition. Without that transition, what went before is minimized or lost. Take a kiss, for instance. A kiss that's ended by a tender look is a totally different experience to one that's ended by the person who kissed you rushing off. To end a conversation with a friendly smile or an "I understand" is different than ending with a strong, abrupt opinion.

The end of every paragraph has a little bit of white space that gives us time to breathe and absorb the paragraph before.

We need that, don't we?

Personally, I don't do well when I'm stressed or feeling hectic. From the beginning of my teaching career I learned that in order for me to progress peacefully and strongly into the next class, I needed to end the previous class with quiet breathing space.

This is not an original idea. Some teachers end their class with a verse that all the children say together. Others end with the quiet of journaling; others with silence, and then a chorused 'goodbye.' I'm always amazed how Waldorf kindergarten teachers can mark each transition with a simple song. The children grow familiar with the song and know when they hear it that they have plenty of time to say goodbye to the doll, to put the wooden blocks back on the shelf, or to start setting the table for snack. They don't have to be told class is over: not a word needs to be said. It's an organic, imitative process, and the children are ready and calmly eager for the next activity.

When it was bedtime for my children I used to sing "Goodnight, My Love" (Ella Fitzgerald's version) as a transition song:

Good night, my love, the quiet old moon is descending
Good night, my love, my moment with you now is ending
It was so heavenly holding you close to me
It will be heavenly to hold you again in a dream…

As soon as my children heard me sing, they knew it was time to brush teeth, put on pajamas, and get ready for a bedtime story.

When you transition, everyone kind of has to transition around you. -Chastity Bono

Writing Practice – Transitions

Transitions in writing require the same quality of moving smoothly from kiss to parting or from playtime to bedtime. Transitional words and phrases help you establish logical, fluid connections within your writing. They help your reader know what you've said and what you're about the say next. They are links, they are the relationship-builders to the ideas in your argument or your story.

They'll also help you organize what you're writing because you'll become clearer about the sequence of what that is. For example, you might start a new paragraph by saying, "Here's another instance when ..."

Or "On the other hand, some people disagree that..." and your reader immediately knows you're going to present an opposing view.

In a short story you might begin a transition to a different scene by placing it in a difference place or a new time. But to keep us fully engaged, you'll want to transition us there. So you'd say, "Several hours later..." or "By the time she arrived night had fallen." What you're doing in transition phrases is summarizing (very briefly) what just happened and then bringing your reader into the next scene or idea.

Here are some examples you can try:

If you're placing your reader in a new timeframe: *afterward, at last, during, meanwhile, sometime later, recently, at the same time.* Avoid "suddenly" since the experience you're conveying by using that word needs to come from the writing itself.

In a new place: overhead there was a…, underneath stood a… , beside her stood…, beyond that was…, near, far away.

Not so often used in fiction, but essential for expository essays, are word-phrases like *consequently, also, in addition to, equally important, furthermore, moreover, nevertheless, on the other hand, indeed.* And when you're illustrating a point use *for example* or *for instance.*

When you're nearing the end, prepare your readers so they aren't surprised: *finally, in conclusion, in the end, on the whole, thus, in summary.*

Leave out phrases that are padding and annoying like "I'd like to add here that…" or "let me just say that…" or (my personal favorite peeve): "Needless to say."

Poetry for transitions:

As a high school teacher, I've chosen to use poetry to transition into the end of class. After the lesson is learned, the homework assignment is given, questions answered, and books put away, the students sit quietly waiting for the anticipated poem. Because I do this regularly, without asking or discussing it with them, it takes only takes a few classes for them to take it for granted. I've found that teenagers appreciate this moment of stillness more than anyone else I know. Some put their heads on their desks and close their eyes while I recite a poem in utter stillness—before the bell rings. Afterwards they remain quiet, and then they move onto the next class, feeling centered and ready instead of frantic.

Why a poem, you might ask? Three reasons:

1) Poetry matters. I think it's important for teens to hear poetry, to hear beautiful language, powerful imagery, and get insights into life and feeling. Many teens I know write poems, but often they get caught up in emotional angst. They need to hear the great poems of the masters too.

2) It's healthy. Listening to poetry is quieting, soothing, harmonious, and that breathing space is good for all of us.

3) I love poetry. I've always loved poems, I can recite many of them by heart. There's nothing I love more than sharing my passion with my students.

I don't know if this is a good idea or a bad one; or whether the kids will remember the poems, or even whether they'll remember that I did this. All I know for sure is that—at the very least—it makes the transition time more pleasant for all of us.

Here is a small list of favorite poets and a suggested poem—but they all wrote dozens of other poems that would work just as well or better. For instance, for a lively class, instead of Eliot's "Prufrock" use one of his "Practical Cats" poems.

If I Could Tell You *by W.H. Auden*
Death Be Not Proud *by John Donne*
The Love Song of J. Alfred Prufrock *by T.S. Eliot*
The Road Not Taken *by Robert Frost*
Hurrahing in Harvest *by Gerald Manly Hopkins*
Ode to Autumn *by John Keats*
The Road Through the Woods *by Rudyard Kipling*
The Secret of the Sea by *H. W. Longfellow*
Annabel Lee by *Edgar Allen Poe*
The Guesthouse *by Rumi*
Ode to the West Wind *by Percy Bysshe Shelley*
Fern Hill *by Dylan Thomas*
Self-portrait *by David Whyte*
This is Just to Say *by William Carlos Williams*

Daily Happinesses

the courage people bring to their lives
flying into the wind
hoping for the best
tulips from Holland
getting angry
sitting on the dune with the seagulls, watching the sun set
curled up on a window seat with a cup of Earl Grey tea

WEEK 42

Draw your chair up close to the edge of the precipice and I'll tell you a story. –F. Scott Fitzgerald

The Ghost Story

The wind blusters and dying leaves fly through swirling mists and falling rain. Dusk envelopes the countryside early; the nights are damp, long, and chilly. In the northern hemisphere, the end of October is a yummy time to conjure up tales that are creepy and mysterious; tales of the dark, the dreary, and the dead.

A long time ago, the Celts celebrated Samhain, their New Year festival, at this time of year. Samhain was one of the most significant annual Druidic festivals, and the celebration lasted for three days. Literally, "samhain" means "summer's end," and the festival marked the end of the light half of the year and the beginning of the dark half. To the ancient druids, the end of the old year was a mystical time when the usual barriers between our world and the otherworld stretched and thinned, allowing contact to be made between human beings and the fairy folk, elemental spirits, and ghosts.

The Celts believed that on the eve of Samhain the spirits of people who had died in that past year would come back to possess living people. On that night all the laws of time and space would be strangely altered, so that the spirits could enter the world of the living.

Scary possibility? The Celts thought so, and on their New Year's Eve they extinguished all fires and lights, so their houses would seem empty and unwelcoming to any roaming spirits. Then they donned strange costumes, many of them dressing up as ghosts and spirits themselves, and paraded through the villages noisily and destructively, so the 'real' spirits would be frightened away. This evolved into our present-day Halloween celebration.

Here's an ancient Irish legend to share around the fire: Jack was a handsome young man, but he was also a drunkard and a prankster. Being clever and arrogant, he decided to play a trick on Satan. He lured Satan to the top of an oak tree, and then carved a cross on the trunk below, trapping Satan in the high branches. But being a good-natured fellow, Jack finally agreed to release Satan, if he promised never to tempt Jack again. Afterward, Jack never drank or played pranks. But when he died, he wasn't allowed to go to Heaven because he'd freed Satan, but neither was he allowed into Hell, because he was so good. Feeling sorry for him, Satan gave him a carved-out turnip with a single glowing ember in it to guide Jack through eternal and frigid darkness. When the Irish came to the United States, they found pumpkins were more common than turnips, and that's how Jack-o-lanterns evolved. So when you carve a pumpkin, think about Jack, who had to wander through an eternity in darkness with only a small glowing turnip to light his way.

Science fiction is no more written for scientists that ghost stories are written for ghosts. –Brian Aldiss

Writing Practice – Write a ghost story.

A ghost story is different from any other kind of story. You are not writing a tale of horror or terror; it is not about werewolves, vampires, or monsters. It is not a fable or a fairy-tale.

There are three essential elements to a ghost story. Most important of all: your ghost story has to be about a ghost. What is a ghost? For the purpose of this exercise, we're going to define a ghost as the spirit of a dead person, one who appears to resemble a person who used to be alive and who haunts a person or place. This spirit may be seen, heard, sensed (usually in a cold clammy sort of way), or may even convey a familiar, eerie fragrance.

Next we come to atmosphere. A ghost story has to be sinister. You need to set a mood that makes the reader or listener shiver and huddle closer to the fire. Think about the drenching rain, the black woods, the crimson leaves, the unexplained creaks, the wail in the tower, the jagged cliffs, the moaning wind on the moors—rich imagery makes all the difference in a ghost story. (Read a tale by Edgar Allen Poe if you want inspiration on how to create spine-chilling atmosphere in a story. *The House of Usher* or *The Tell-Tale Heart* are classics.)

The idea of a ghost—a dead person wandering around your lonely mansion—is pretty unnerving, and your redolently creepy atmosphere is also ominous. Now you need to come up with a plot that's intriguing and terrifying. In your story your ghost has to have a purpose, a raison d'etre, if you will. In order for the ghost to eventually depart, it must have concluded a task: of revenge, consolation, or something you yourself come up with. Again, this does not entail horror, gore, violence. It's more frightening than that, more deeply puzzling and mysterious.

That's all there is to it: atmosphere, a ghost, and a purpose. Remember, in writing a ghost story you're trying to scare your readers out of their wits. You want them to tremble as they carry their candle up the stairs when they go to bed. You want them to quiver and quake under the covers when they confuse the wind rattling the window panes for footsteps in the attic. You want them to shriek in terror when a door slams unexpectedly in another part of the house.

It is wonderful that five thousand years have now elapsed since the creation of the world, and still it is undecided whether or not there has ever been an instance of the spirit of any person appearing after death. All argument is against it; but all belief is for it. –Samuel Johnson

Daily Happinesses

thin mist swirling over a lake
hickory nuts hurled to the ground
The Day of the Dead
gazing into a mirror at the stroke of midnight
crimson poison ivy
belladonna
candles dripping down the sides and sputtering into dark

WEEK 43

The most valuable of all talents is that of never using two words when one will do. –Thomas Jefferson

Murder your darlings

Writing requires skill, as does painting, or playing an instrument. You practice and practice, and eventually phrases, sentences, words, paragraphs, and eventually chapters and books take on a life of their own, because you don't have to figure out how to finger a chord or shade a cloud; you *know* it.

Skill in any artistic form leaves the artist free. That's the point of learning a skill—it's to free the artist inside you to be able to create.

If I handed you a guitar and said, "play it—you're so talented musically" and you never practiced scales, chords, music, learning songs, you would always be frustrated. Unfree. If you learn how to play it, though, you become confident and free to improvise, to enjoy, and eventually create great music. Skill doesn't just 'happen' all by itself.

I'm continually floored when I'm asked to read work written by either teens or grown-ups, and I point out an egregious grammatical error or confused thinking, and their response is: "But I *like* it that way."

Fair enough. But it's not going to serve you to like something unless you know what error you're making or the fact that your thinking is confused.

One of the best pieces of advice I ever received was George Bernard Shaw's famous "Murder your darlings." If there's a part of your piece that you are particularly attached to—so attached that a teacher or editor advising you to cut it out brings tears of rage to your eyes—then chances are you should cut it out. The more enraged you feel, the more likely it should be gotten rid of.

This is not necessarily because it's a lousy sentence or scene; sometimes it's because it doesn't fit where you've placed it.

So save it. I have a fat folder I call "Darlings." Ruthlessly, I bury them alive—and maybe I'll let them out some day.

Put down everything that comes into your head and then you're a writer. But an author is one who can judge his own stuff's worth, without pity, and destroy most of it. -Colette

Writing Practice—Edit, edit, edit.

Have someone read something you wrote that you 'love.' It should be someone fairly objective, like a teacher or editor. Someone who knows correct grammar, clarity in writing, logic—as well as what you're trying to accomplish. Every writer needs a mentor, a teacher, an editor—someone to help them continue to hone their skills. A writing critique group, for instance, is one of the best (and free).

Try to be open to what your critiquer says. Don't bristle; close your eyes and *listen*. Then let the response you got rest quietly for a few days before reading your piece again, with just a bit more detachment and clarity.

Editing is a different skill to writing. Editing is left-brain thinking. It's analyzing structure, word usage, sequence, clarity. If you're new to the editing process, it helps to have a check list beside you and in the beginning you may have to go through the piece of writing more than once. Here are four things you could pay particular attention to the next time you're editing your manuscript:

Continuity: One of the main flaws an editor can pick up on is what is referred to in the film world as "continuity." Especially in a novel, when you've probably gone through a countless number of revisions, it's more than likely that you have forgotten that the last time two people spoke it was Sunday, not Thursday. Or when she woke up that morning in the middle of a steaming hot jungle she was wearing a red dress and she's had no opportunity to change into something blue.

Dialog: Often I find in the heart of the story authors are in a hurry to move to a scene that they are more inspired by. Instead of filling out the moment with dialog, they'll tell us what the characters talked about and then quickly move on. It rarely works in a tense situation—we need to be right with the action not being pulled back. Better to leave out the fact they even had a conversation than to tell us what they said but don't give us the privilege of hearing it.

Word usage: is that really the best word you can use? An editor can spot a word that you're reaching for but haven't quite found a mile away. Thesauruses are the bane of a writer oftentimes—I can usually tell immediately when it's been used. Of course you can use it, but only if you're looking for a specific word that's at the tip of pen and you recognize it in the Thesaurus. It's not a place to browse for a word because more often than not you decide you "like" a word, but it doesn't usually fit.

Simplify. Editors can help writers simplify their thoughts. This brings clarity and precision to the writing practice. Don't use two words when one will suffice. Don't be convoluted in your thinking. Say what you mean. Describe the scene beautifully but simply and clearly.

Lean to be your own editor.

Prune what is turgid, elevate what is commonplace, arrange what is disorderly, introduce rhythm where the language is harsh, modify where it is too absolute.
-Marcus Fabius Quintilianus, circa 65 A.D.

Daily Happinesses

climbing into the chilly tree house and being alone
soft, warm socks
the silence of the desert
swimming in a mountain lake in autumn
the first frost
late afternoon sun on pine needles
piles of root vegetables on a kitchen counter

November

WEEK 44

"There is no need to be ashamed of tears, for tears bear witness that a man has the greatest of courage, the courage to suffer." –Victor Frankl

Nyai Loro Kidul

When I was a girl and traveling around the world on a freighter with my family, we sailed through the Straits of Malacca and paused in Singapore to unload our cargo of copra. There we took a sampan into the city and found an elegant, red-and-gold restaurant where we ordered the specialty: sarang burung, or bird's nest soup.

As we ate, this is what the waiter told us: edible bird's nests are made by the little sea swallows of Indonesia. These are harvested from the ocean three times a year. Using coconut-fiber ropes, young men climb down the sheer cliff onto a ledge high above the rough waves, carrying empty sacks with them. There they wait on a wobbly rope platform for just the right wave to approach. When they see one, they leap into it, clutching their sacks, and are swept *under* the ledge on which they had been standing. They are washed into a dark cave where they scrabble and fumble around the slippery walls, seeking the bird's nests.

When they're ready to return, they have to time it just right, or the violent waves will crush them against the cliff, or they'll be swept out to sea.

Nyai Loro Kidul, the goddess of the South Seas, is the patron goddess of the bird's-nest gatherers. Briefly, her legend (one of many) is that she was the wife of the king of Java, and a rival wife became jealous and put a spell on her that made her horrifically ugly with a skin disease. In despair, she fled the palace and wandered to the ocean where she dreamed that if she leapt into the waves she would be cured and would regain her beauty. This she did, and the spirits and demons of the sea crowned her the Spirit-Queen of the South Seas. From her dwelling place in the heart of the ocean she controls the waves and tides of the oceans around her.

She is sometimes depicted as a mermaid with a tail; other times the lower part of her body is a snake.

She is also wife to the Sultan of Yogyakart, known as the "Great Mountain," whom she visits once a year to consummate their relationship.

Curiosity will conquer fear even more than bravery will. -James Stephens

Writing Practice: Be Brave

As a writer—or any creator—you have experienced times when you feel stuck. You don't know how you can move forward in your project or get out of your rut. Try to imagine your stuckness as the skin of a snake that you've outgrown. Your writer's block is your not-so-easy process of shedding the skin that no longer serves you. Nyai Loro Kidul's skin disease brought her to the brink of despair, until she learned how to jump into the stormy waves, and was not just healed but crowned queen of the seas. She had shed the skin that no longer served her.

Another aspect of Nyai Loro Kidul's mythology is her ability to change shape several times a day. This is something you as a writer do as well: you take on the shape of one character, and then another. If you are trying to paint the wind in the pines or a rider galloping across the moor, you take on the shape of the wind—or you become the horse. You *are* the magic.

When you're feeling that your skin is too tight, try something new. This is a good time to venture in a different direction. Take a break from the 'shoulds' and 'musts' and deadlines and self-imposed word counts. Do something daring and different. Write a song instead of an article. Get out your water-colors instead of counting how many pages you wrote today. Try extricating yourself from a skin that's too tight by wriggling into a previously unexplored and potentially scary activity.

Nyai Loro Kidul is not a benevolent goddess: she'll take the soul of any one she wants. Let her. Fishermen are scared of her, and you should be too. But that doesn't mean you shouldn't fish—that's your life. Instead, it means you should throw yourself into the ocean of Writing and let yourself drown in it, come what may. Be like the bird's nest gatherers. Be brave.

Happiness is a form of courage. –Holbrook Jackson

Daily Happinesses

alyssum still blooming in November
the scent of cedar in an old chest
Islamic tiles in a walled garden
breathing your lover's breath
sailing into a hidden harbor for a rest
the pyramids at Giza
fire sparks from a bonfire

WEEK 45

I often think of a poem as a door that opens into a room where I want to go. -Minnie Bruce Pratt

Creating a poem

During the November full moon—called Frost Moon, or Beaver Moon, and in some places (probably farther north) Snow Moon by some Native American tribes—a poet-friend and I decided to try to collaborate on a poem together. He lives near the beach in Florida and I live in the mountains of New England; he is a mixed-media story-telling artist; I am, at heart, a writer of romantic novels. Oh, one more thing: we've never met.

Our plan was this: at 9:15 in the evening, at the exact moment when the moon was 'full' (which only happens for a minute or so) we would go outside and look at the moon. We were going to create a mutual poem.

The word 'poetry' comes from the Greek word *poesis,* which means a "making." In a poem, language and meaning combine to create a work of art.

What do we mean when we speak of 'language'? We think of language as consisting of words, but language is also gesture, expression, code, symbol. One thing I learned from this experience of collaboration is that a poem lies in its relationship to the person who experiences it as much as to the one who creates it.

As Mike stood in his balmy ocean breeze, listening to the rustling waves breaking on the smooth, quiet beach, I dug my way through waist-high leaves that swirled in a chilly north wind, listening to the coyotes barking on the hill. But the moon at which we both gazed together was the same moon.

I wrote a poem based on the experience, but when I was done I realized that the shared experience itself was the poem.

Poetry is just the evidence of life. If your life is burning well, poetry is just the ash. -Leonard Cohen

Writing Practice – Sound Translations

This is a technique that can inspire you to write and also to set you free from self-imposed pressure to produce a perfect poem.

Find a poem written in a language that is unfamiliar to you. Examine the words, the lines, imagine the rhythm, and create a homophonic translation—in other words, using words that you think might be the right translation, based on how the words sound.

You'll find that by doing this, poetic language is simply a way to express a feeling, thought, insight, or experience.

Here's an excerpt you could try translating from the Old Norse *Hávamál*, part of Odin's rune song.

Veit ec at ec hecc vindga meiði a
netr allar nío,
geiri vndaþr oc gefinn Oðni,

sialfr sialfom mer,
a þeim meiþi, er mangi veit, hvers hann af rótom renn.

Við hleifi mic seldo ne viþ hornigi,
nysta ec niþr,
nam ec vp rvnar,
opandi nam,
fell ec aptr þaðan.

Or if you prefer Latin, here's something written by Virgil:

Excudent allii spirantia mollius aera
(credo equidem),
vivos ducent de marmore vultus, orabunt causas melius,
caelique meatus describent radio et surgentia sidera dicent:
tu regere imperio populos, Romane,
memento
(hae tibi erunt artes),
pacisque imponere morem,
parcere subiectis
et debellare superbos.

Find your own! Remember, you're not trying to translate the actual words but to be inspired by the sounds of the words.

Poetry is nearer to vital truth than history. –Plato

Daily Happinesses

talking earnestly with a friend
unusual colors in fabrics
The Queen of Sheba
an evening with a group of comedians
the music of the spheres
forgiveness
breaking into laughter at the same time

WEEK 46

The secret to humor is surprise. –Aristotle

What makes people laugh?

There are all sorts of ways: Sarcasm, slapstick, irony, teasing. Puns. Visual gags.

Everyone's funny bone is tickled in different ways.

Here are ten ways to humor up your own writing:

"That's so true." This is a technique used by cartoonists and many stand-up comedians. They take a typical situation and describe it exactly as it is—thus bringing to attention to its outrageousness or silliness. Jerry

Seinfeld has his audience in stitches when he says: "Have you ever noticed that..." So, be observant—look around you—and notice things. Before long you'll get used to seeing many situations in a humorous light.

Ouch. What's funnier: someone slipping on a banana peel or someone hugging a friend? Slapstick can hurt, but it works.

Dissing someone. So strange to think that being disrespectful or mean to a friend is funny, but if you count the number of times you laugh at rude or sarcastic comments made in a typical sit-com, you'll see that it's the case.

Exaggerated situation. Writing about something in your everyday life might not be very funny, but if it's exaggerated it usually is. For example, maybe your character works in a factory. *Yawn*. But if that factory makes chocolate bonbons and the conveyor belt starts moving faster and faster as your character tries to keep up, and the chocolate starts going everywhere, including into her mouth, you'll definitely inspire chuckles.

Exaggerated language. Use words that are unusual or funny-sounding. Robert Beard recently published a book called *The 100 Funniest Words in English*. Here are some examples: *abibliophobia* (the fear of running out of reading material);***batrachomyomachy*** (making a mountain out of a molehill); ***bloviate*** (to speak pompously or brag); ***borborygm*** (a rumbling of the stomach); ***collop*** (a slice of meat or fold of flab);***formication*** (the sense of ants crawling on your skin); and my favorite of all: ***gastromancy*** (telling your fortune from the rumblings of your stomach).

Use detail. Instead of writing "she held up the bracelet in front of him," try writing "tantalizing diamonds dripped before his bugged-out eyes."

Timing and structure matters. In other words, don't tell the punch line first.

Puns: Personally, I laugh hardest at word slip-ups, puns, and those widely-circulated Engrish errors that crop up in various websites nowadays. The bear who goes into a bar and eats, shoots, and leaves makes me smile just because of a misplaced comma.

Confuse. Juxtaposing imagery in a surreal way can be funny. Remember Monte Python's Hell's Grannies? The not-so-funny Hell's Angels became dear little old ladies on loud motorcycles who beat up unfortunates with their umbrellas. Yes, we laughed. Turn a situation on its head.

Surprise. Come up with an unexpected punchline. Imagine the possibilities and then surprise us with something we never thought of ourselves. Ask yourself: *"What if…?"*

A person without a sense of humor is like a wagon without springs. It's jolted by every pebble on the road. –Harriet Beecher Stowe

Writing Practice – Make someone laugh

Get in the habit of writing at least one "Have you ever noticed how…" sentence a day.

Write at least one "What-if" each day. What if this was the situation, what if this was happening, what if something was this way.

Think in puns: Get into the habit of thinking "what else could this word mean?"

Notice what makes you laugh and write it down.

Set yourself the goal of making at least one person laugh every day.

Ultimately, though, this is your ideal (as the wise Abraham Maslow suggests): to direct your sense of humor at yourself or the human condition rather than at the expense of someone else.

Humor is reason gone mad. –Groucho Marx

Daily Happinesses

a fresh cord of wood delivered
castles in Bavaria
the eye of love
meeting at Galleon's Lap
sorting clothes and giving them away
a stranger from Brazil
the dried corn stalks in the fields

WEEK 47

I would maintain that thanks are the highest form of thought; and that gratitude is happiness doubled by wonder. –G.K. Chesterton

Worship Privately, Rejoice Together

Although Thanksgiving appears to be a uniquely American holiday, the mood of late November in the northern hemisphere feels hectic, festive, familyish—and it sometimes can feel dark. Very few holidays are not based in some way on seasonal or pagan rituals—whether they are secular, as is Thanksgiving, or religious. In northern climates (in days long ago), this might be the last time you could see families and friends till spring. In agricultural civilizations, it's the celebration of the end of harvest. It's okay to feast now; by February there may be very little left. Nowadays we don't have that worry; instead the anxiety has crept inwards, and emerges as family-related issues: passionate reunions, guilt, or nostalgia. This time of year can be fraught with tension, excitement, friendliness, food, warmth, light, depression, and so on.

I was eighteen when I first moved to the United States after having lived abroad since I was two. Experiencing my first Thanksgiving here, I was cynical. Like the dubious celebration of Guy Fawkes Day in England, Thanksgiving seemed historical propaganda with little resonance of either spirit or nature. My cynicism increased over the years: with so many starving people in the world, to overeat seemed gross. To slaughter millions of turkeys on one day felt like a bloodbath. Family tensions, hurt feelings, exhausting travel, hours of watching football on television ... ugh ugh *ugh*.

As my children grew up, I emphasized the harvest festival aspect of Thanksgiving, making it a universal theme rather than distinctly American. It was a pleasant opportunity to see grandparents. It was fun to cook together. Having grown up in many countries around the world, I introduced un-traditional traditions. Greek dolmades. Delicious Italian vegetarian lasagna. Home-made sushi made by my son when he was working at a Japanese restaurant. Baked curry tofu made by my vegetarian daughter. We nodded to the Massachusetts tradition of squash and cranberries, but more because these were local to our state than because they were a tradition. I was always trying to make our holidays global.

Then one day I was browsing in our local library and found a children's book about the first Thanksgiving. As I read it, I was struck by revelation. Whether or not this story actually happened doesn't matter, because it's 'true' in the real sense of the word. This is what I learned:

Planning for the first Thanksgiving was contentious. Tables were set up, banquet-style, along the main street, and the food was—at last—abundant and delicious. However, no celebration could take place without first saying prayers, giving thanks, and offering a grace. Many of the pilgrims had made the decision to leave their homes and loved ones far across the sea in order to find a place where they could worship freely. Religion mattered deeply to them. But unfortunately there were several different religions represented by those pilgrims who had survived their first year in New England.

According to the history I read, they began to bicker about the form of prayer, and then to argue vehemently. The arguments escalated, and it looked as though the feast that was planned would be tainted by the very quality the pilgrims had sought to leave behind: intolerance for another's right to worship as one pleased.

The contentious meetings were resolved this way: the wise elders of the small Plymouth colony like William Bradford and Edward Winslow declared that every person or family would go inside their own houses and worship privately. Only then would they emerge and the feasting and partying would be done together.

Now, to me, Thanksgiving is one of the loveliest of all American traditions. Not to neglect the spirituality, the seasonal significance, and the reverence of a holiday, but to choose it independently, to practice it privately, and then to rejoice together, with family and friends.

Writing Practice – Thank You

One thing I know about this time of year: most of us are too busy to write anything coherent.

So, try this: the last thing at night before you turn off your light or first thing in the morning before you turn it on, write a list titled "Thank you."

Thank you for .... it's another way of counting blessings. Be surreal though, too, in this exercise. Surprise yourself. Thank yourself for things that you think you're not grateful for; like a leaky faucet (that brings mindfulness) or an angry telephone call (that let's your own anger flow out, instead of being pent up inside). These are all unseen guests from beyond—don't assume you already know why an annoyance or sadness has come into your life. Greet them all—welcome them all in, at this thanksgiving time.

If the only prayer you said in your whole life was "thank you," that would suffice. –Meister Eckhart

Daily Happinesses

cobalt blue glass
taking off your shoes when entering
a big bear hug
saying goodbye and closing the door
the birth of the white bison
the stranger taking your hand and leading you out of there
kissing the inside of her wrists

December

Week 48 – Does it matter?
Week 49 – Observation
Week 50 – Three wishes
Week 51 – Pictures, scissors, glue
Week 52 – Janusian thinking

WEEK 48

A scrupulous writer, in every sentence that he writes, will ask himself at least four questions, thus:

1. *What am I trying to say?*
2. *What words will express it?*
3. *What image or idiom will make it clearer?*
4. *Is this image fresh enough to have an effect?*

–George Orwell, Politics and the English Language,

Does it Matter?

One of the best bits of writing advice I ever got was from my brother who, at the time he gave it, was involved in theater design. He told me that everything single thing I wrote in my novel had to be relevant to the character or the plot.

Now, this may seem obvious to most of you, but how often do you ruthlessly pare your novel so that *nothing* that isn't relevant to character development or the story survives?

Okay, in the novel he was reading (and, in my defense, this was a long, long time ago), I dressed one of my characters in "brown pants and a yellow shirt." My brother couldn't figure out the kind of person I was describing. Someone with terrible fashion sense? Or someone in disguise?

Or did the character like yellow because he was a cheerful sort of person—in which case, why the brown pants? Was he a delivery man?

The fact that this character was introduced during a cruise cocktail party made that unlikely.

I couldn't defend the clothes I picked. Ever since then I've dressed my characters in clothes appropriate to their personality. I've also made sure that I've given them props in their rooms or offices that matter to their stories. Every single thing matters.

I never knew what was meant by choice of words. It was one word or none. -Robert Frost

Writing Practice – Your Jewel Box

There are many ways to enhance your stories or articles by using details that may appear arbitrary, but that infuse your character with personality or subtly play on our emotions.

For example, use color to describe temperament. If a character has a hot temper, dress her in red.

If she's a calm sort of type, make sure she's got a blue head band on.

Use flavor or fragrance to describe mood. The delicate, elusive fragrance of violets is different to the headiness of sweet jasmine. If there's tension and fear, make sure there's something bitter around or something metal.

Weather is a fabulous way to create emotion. Thunderstorms are classic examples, a serene summer day is another. But you can get more descriptive and evoke the situation much more vividly by describing heat and chill, night or day, clouds, stars, and the quality of the earth beneath your feet.

Details make all the difference. Here's an aspect many writers overlook: jewelry. Take a look at what kind of jewelry your protagonist is wearing. An emerald pinky ring? Do diamonds drip from her ear lobes? A simple gold wedding band? Something rare and extraordinary, like alexandrite? Gemstones have strong vibrations and are known for the influence they have on the wearer. So use them to describe your character.

Here are a few descriptions I've come up with that you can use to enhance your character's personality (most of these are from research that I did when I wrote "A Perfect Gem"):

If your character wears jasper he or she might be a powerful healer. Jasper is a stone of courage and independence. It is known for its ability to ease stress and to bring emotional stability. All jaspers—no matter what color—balance your energy and protect from fear and negativity, making you feel relaxed and secure.

Pearls symbolize emotional balance and tranquility. Usually pale white or cream-colored, pearls can also be found in dark blue, gray, and even black. A character who wears them may seem serene and traditional—pearls can also be used to ease stress and irritation, so someone who's trying to calm down could reach for her pearls.

Peridot, a light green gem of the springtime, can be used to open new doors. It also helps in relieving stress, anxiety, and guilt, and to activate personal growth. Your character could use it to protect against negativity or depression.

Carnelian is an energy-booster. With its deep red to red-orange hue, the stone is associated with wealth and nobility. Hold a carnelian and feel your energy increase. Carnelian helps remove insecurities so that your character's inner light can shine out and be seen by others. It also brings out qualities of humor and calm.

Amber also has soothing and warming properties. If you're seeking a way to bring more joy into your character's life, use amber—it will bring him lightness and equilibrium.

Turquoise is the symbol of friendship, as well as a symbol of wealth. One of the oldest protection amulets, it can be used to overcome shyness or over-sensitivity. It brings peace to the home and wisdom to the wearer. Your character can wear it to heal feelings of despair and sadness.

Citrine is known as the lucky "merchants' stone." It can increase self-esteem, protect from negative energy, open your mind to new thoughts and opportunities, and bring love and joy in the process.

Jade strengthens your mental agility and clarity of reason. Use it to bring you happiness, to attract love, and even money: its prosperous energy will help when you are contemplating your next plan of action. It is also a protective stone, guarding against accidents and misfortune.

Use the brilliant aquamarine to show someone who has tremendous courage and strength. This gem also symbolizes happiness in relationships. Aquamarine can be used to inspire trust, harmony, and friendship. Sailors believed it would protect them on their sea voyages.

Deep red garnets symbolize good health, faithfulness, and imagination. They can help make a business successful, and they are excellent travel protectors. They bring constancy to friendships. Above all, the garnet is a stone of purity, truth, and compassion. What your character learns from using garnets may be difficult, but it will strengthen her inwardly.

Diamonds vibrate with purity, harmony, and love, and bring abundance and prosperity.

Rubies inspire energy, ardor, and power. You can use these fiery gems to ignite strong passion in your character.

The deep blue of lapis lazuli shimmers with golden pyrites. A stone of friendship and truth, it encourages harmony in relationships and the wearer to be authentic and honest. It strengthens self-awareness and creativity. Because of its high vibrational intensity, it needs to be used only with sincere love and wisdom.

Amethyst can transform energy and instill inner peace, wisdom, and healing. Place an amethyst in a sunlit window to dispel negativity in the home. Place it in moonlight and everyone will feel calmer. Amethyst helps overcome fears and cravings and even helps relieve headaches. It is a stone of friendship.

Sapphires stir feelings of sympathy and harmony, friendship and loyalty. They'll help your character find expression for her deepest soul longings.

Emeralds vibrate with emotion. They help to attract wealth, to make dreams come true, and act as a symbol of hope. A gem of prophecy, reason, and wisdom, emeralds can be used to heal the physical heart, as well as to bring true love.

Extremely rare, alexandrite is one of the hardest gemstones in existence. It changes color depending on the light: it can be pale red or red-purple, or green or blue-green depending on the time of day. It also changes from violet to green, or from pale azure to gold. Use this magical crystal to open your character's heart, to build her self-esteem and self-confidence. It brings spiritual love, joy, great good fortune, and opens the way to knowing one's higher self.

A word is not a crystal, transparent and unchanged; it is the skin of a living thought and may vary greatly in color and content according to the circumstances and time in which it is used. –Oliver Wendell Holmes, Jr.

Daily Happinesses

sunshine on the pomegranate tree
that long talk with a fox in a field
wintry mix outside while you're in bed
dipping your bare feet into an icy stream
not spending money
climbing through the cloud forests of the Andes
the stones moving at dusk in Avebury

WEEK 49

"It's not what you look at that matters,
it's what you see." –*Henry David Thoreau*

A sense of wonder

There's something wondrous about the first snowfall. There's something gentle, and promising, and utterly beautiful. It's like magic, the way it curls around branches, and lightly captures and blanches small objects that were previously dull and drab.

When the first snow falls, there's almost always an intense emotional glee attached to it. We can't help but be entranced, even awed by the quiet, the change from brown to white in the landscape around.

How do you describe it, though? How can you show its beauty, its quiet, its quality of wonder, rather than just tell us "the snow was beautiful. Everything seemed very quiet."

The secret to showing not telling often lies in the *observation*. In order to write with clarity and precision, it's crucial to exercise your powers of observation (not limiting that word to your sense of sight). The practice of writing down exactly what you see and smell and hear pulls you out of your self-absorption without deadening your passion and interest in yourself and your response to the falling snow.

We write because we think; we also think because we write.

Thinking is not limited to the important aspects of writing such as parts of speech, correct punctuation, thesis statement. Thinking is also imagination and being open to the possibility. Training the powers of observation—

including fragrances, sounds, tastes—is the foundation of science and art. And, in my opinion, of education.

Albert Einstein happens to be related to my uncle-by-marriage, Konrad Kellen. Konrad told me a story once: When he was thirteen, he was taking a walk with Albert Einstein in the woods on his estate outside of Berlin. Konrad, a brilliant and philosophical boy, felt strongly enough about Einstein's relativity theory, and decided he had to tell him why he did not think it could be true. After he had finished his outburst, they walked on for a long time, in absolute silence, while Konrad felt smaller and smaller at having dared to argue with the great man.

At last Einstein stopped, turned to him, and said slowly, "You may be right. And if you find out that you are right, I want you to come and tell me before you tell anyone else, because I will be very interested."

I'm telling this story because I think the essence of Albert Einstein's greatness is not only his imagination and brilliance, but his acute observation and his openness to all the possibilities.

The important thing is not to stop questioning. Curiosity has its own reason for existing. -Albert Einstein

<u>*Writing Practice – Observation*</u>

Practice observation, and writing down what you observe. Choose a window to sit next to, and try to do this exercise at the same time every day for at least a week.

Describe the view outside your window. In the beginning, it may seem simple and bland. A tree, a roof, a street. But as you begin to describe the scene, and then return to it in various moods and kinds of weather, your "seeing" eye comes to play, and you begin to do a strange and thrilling dance, even with something as mundane as a familiar view outside your window.

This exercise is similar to an artist's practice of painting or drawing a still-life.

You're not including your mood in this exercise. Don't say "I love the way the cars are parked so cozily together." Instead write, "Cars—black, silver, white, and one red one—are parked cozily together, nose to tail."

Engage metaphors, alliteration, assonance—create a mood using the sound of our language and stretching your imagination to include images not normally connected with your scene.

I recommend this writing practice as an ongoing exercise. You may want to vary the scene every few weeks or so or even set up a still-life of your own.

We can't solve problems by using the same kind of thinking we used when we created them. -Albert Einstein

Daily Happinesses

piles of silk and satin pillows
reindeer in Lapland
getting into a warm car on a cold night
fragrance of Mediterranean fig
transcendence at the bottom of the sky
the blueness of the sky against newly fallen snow
sweeping away the cobwebs

WEEK 50

It seems to me we can never give up longing and wishing while we are thoroughly alive. There are certain things we feel to be beautiful and good, and we must hunger after them. –George Eliot

Three Wishes

When you make a wish, where does that wish really come from? Where does it go?

Imagine that you really did find that magic lamp, or the talking flounder, or a mysterious ring... and you were able to wish for whatever you wanted. What would it be?

You might begin with the desire for something personal and important to you in the moment. A new car, or a good job, perhaps.

Then you mull and mull, perhaps you sleep with the lamp under your pillow ... and you wake up reflecting on the fact that, if you had only one wish, perhaps you'd better wish that your son gets accepted to college or Aunt Edna pulls through that operation... This kind of wish can become emotional and intense when you think about all the people in the world you love and care about want to help.

Mulling still longer, chances are you'll tell yourself that, given a once-in-a-lifetime opportunity like this one, you'd better make a difference to the world at large. What would you choose: No more hungry children? Save the whales? End war for all time?

Wishes are born way deep inside you, and go out into the world as we know it, creating goodwill and spreading love. Ultimately, the outcome doesn't matter. There's always something to be learned from making a wish, because making a wish is not as simple as it may at first appear. The magic lamp must be used with care. The generous flounder does its best to give the fisherman's wife her heart's desire, but it is not enough. The monkey's paw is possibly the most troubling manifestation of a wish imaginable. Making a wish often leads to trouble.

Making a wish is another lens through which we as writers can experience life.

Be as you wish to seem. –Socrates

Writing Practice – Three Kinds of Wishes

- wishing for something for one's self;
- wishing for something for someone else;
- wishing for something for the world at large.

Part 1: Make a wish for yourself.

Write a fairytale that includes your opportunity to make three wishes. Think about these wishes carefully—they should be things you want for yourself very, very much.

In order to relax and enjoy your way into this practice, write in a fairy-tale style. Begin with "Once upon a time ..." and end fairly traditionally. In between, enjoy the details: the silks and satins, the rubies and emeralds, the archetypal characters, the magic lake. Elaborate on three wishes that you yourself would choose, if you were given the chance, and imagine what would happen if those three wishes came true.

State each wish as you move through the story—and why is it important to you.

Describe what happens once it is granted.

End with the consequence.

Part 2: Make a wish for someone else.

In order to do this exercise you need to step outside yourself and imagine what it must be like to be someone else. You need to be quiet and go inwards, in order to go outwards.

But don't limit yourself to something you think your friend 'needs.' Imagine something grand—this is a once-in-a-lifetime opportunity. Perhaps you think he or she should be able to understand the language of animals! Or fly to the moon! Or maybe it's a hand-carved toy train set... Try to get into their hearts to think about this exercise. Then write a short description of who the person is for whom you're giving this wish, and include your connection.

Precede your wish with an introduction: "I have a dream for you..." or "In all my wanderings, I searched high and low, and found this..." or "I shot an arrow into the air..."

Part 3:Make a wish for the world.

Holiday wishes often fall into this category: "Peace on Earth" or "Joy to the World."

What are the themes that you are concerned about at this time of year? What charities move you the most? Do you wish you could cure blindness? What about all those puppies and kittens at a shelter you saw—would you like to see them all adopted in the next few days?

Get a piece of paper and write out your wishes. As you begin, you'll see that the phrases begin to flow on to the page. Make them in arcs, and upside down, and use dashes and exclamation marks and little doodles to decorate them. Fill out the page with your wishes as though they are beautiful snowflakes.

Things don't change, but by and by our wishes change. -Marcel Proust

Daily Happinesses

the shapes of letters
fresh oranges
holding hands in the dark
ostriches looking over the fence
Giotto
a sackful of handmade toys
talking with tree frogs

WEEK 51

Creativity is a drug I cannot live without. -Cecil B. DeMille

Pictures, scissors, glue

The week between Christmas and New Year's is a peculiar one. Some of my friends are in Florida, basking in the sunshine. Our president typically goes to beautiful Oahu, where I love to imagine him in peaceful sunshine, with the trade winds to soothe and rejuvenate. I have friends from long ago who still gather every year at the castle they own on the west coast of Scotland. Still others are stacking wood for their wood stoves and cozying up in intimate family togetherness. Others are partying and feasting in the city.

What are you doing?

What do you wish you were doing?

It may be just too hard to write this week. This feels like an out-of-kilter time, this week just before the New Year kicks in, and before we're back to the routine of daily life.

So instead of writing, try this instead:

Writing Practice: Craft time.

Creativity can be described as letting go of certainties. -Gail Sheehy

Collect some magazines, catalogues, or holiday cards—ones with lots of photographs of things like country homes, city fun, architecture, food, people, vacations, gardens, sports.

Sit at a comfy spot with scissors, glue, and a great big piece of cardstock paper. Begin cutting out all those photos that appeal to you—the ones that jump out at you. Is it the blue of a Caribbean beach? Buttery suede boots striding along a city sidewalk? A chocolate cake? Whatever it is, cut it out and place it (don't glue yet) on your backing. When you've cut plenty of pictures and they're piled high in front of you, begin arranging them. Try to make a cohesive picture rather than random placement. See what emerges as you play with the images. What is interesting to me is how unique my selection and outcome is—I always imagine that everyone would select the same photographs as me, but that's not how this exercise works. It's actually a visualization of how you see yourself and you are creating a world that, in some form or other, heals, encourages, and inspires.

Enjoy the process—and then glue the result so you can look at it again, especially next year, at this same time.

A writer is working when he's staring out of the window. –Burton Rascoe

Daily Happinesses

playing cards on a train
the smell of fresh ground dark roast coffee
guests washing dishes
waving a magic wand
holding a mirror up to the sky
swimming to the underwater pyramid at Yonaguni-Jima, Japan
a half-open yellow rose

WEEK 52

The curious paradox is that when I accept myself just as I am, then I can change. -Carl Rogers

Janusian thinking

Studies involving fifty or so Nobel prize winners in physiology, chemistry, medicine and physics, as well as Pulitzer Prize-winning writers and other artists, reveal a surprising similarity in their creative process.

Called 'Janusian thinking' after the Roman god Janus, it involves holding two opposing ideas or images in your mind at the same time. The researchers conclude most major scientific breakthroughs and artistic masterpieces occur through the process of formulating antithetical ideas and then trying to resolve them.

Janus was the Roman god of gates and doors, bridges, openings and closings, beginnings and endings, past and future. Represented by an image of two heads, each looking in opposite directions, this unusual god was worshipped at seasonal markers such as planting and harvesting, at beginnings such as marriage and birth, and even historical epochs, such as the transition from primitive to civilized cultures. Janus's namesake, the month of January, describes the gift he had of being able to see into the future as well as into the past—a gift he was given by the god Saturn. At midnight, on the last day of the year, he looks back at the old year, and at the same moment he looks forward into the new. That's not easy to do! We get lost in nostalgia for the past and longing for the future—try being in both at the same time. (It's not necessarily 'being here now.')

Here's an example of Janusian (or paradoxical) thinking: The physicist Niels Bohr imagined that light could be analyzed as either a wave or as a particle, but never simultaneously as both. He had to hold both concepts in his head at the same time in order to conceive his principle of complementarity in quantum theory.

Einstein recalls how he first conceived his theory of relativity: "For an observer in free fall from the roof of a house, there exists, during his fall, no gravitational field in his immediate vicinity. If the observer releases any objects, they will remain, relative to him, in a state of rest." Falling and being still—at the same time. It *is* possible!

Some of the best descriptive metaphors you'll read are Janusian: Keats describes April rain that "fosters the droop-headed flowers" and "hides the green hill in a shroud' at the same time—life and death in the same imagery. Powerful.

An artistic example of Janusian thinking are those extraordinary artistic renderings by M.C. Escher, who draws, for example, cubes that are paradoxical—they can be visually 'seen' either as protruding or receding.

Practice looking at a cube in this way, and trying to regard it from either perspective. Just an exercise this simple will help your decision-making skills as well as loosen up your imagination. You are, literally, thinking 'outside the box.' There's no better exercise for a writer than to free yourself from the constraints of what is expected, clichéd, outworn, one-sided. Anything that seems impossible is bound to challenge and thrill anyone who writes fiction.

You're reaching beyond the obvious—and that's the essence of being creative. Janusian thinking—holding two diametrically opposing views in your mind at the same time—is like gold to writers.

Every experience is a paradox in that it means to be absolute, and yet is relative; in that it somehow always goes beyond itself and yet never escapes itself. –T. S. Eliot

Writing Practice –Janusian writing

Think of something, and ask yourself: "What is the opposite of this?" Then try to imagine both opposites existing at the same time.

In writing a story you do this all the time. A character holds passion and hatred for an unfaithful wife in his heart at the same time. A young, angry boy may long to run away from home, but his love for his family keeps him captive at the same time. Warring emotions in characters are Janusian qualities: you might feel both pity and bitterness when you see an enemy fail. Or both disappointment and relief when something exciting and scary doesn't happen. And of course there's always the pain and the pleasure of unrequited love.

Choose a theme for a poem or a story: for example, envy, or summertime, or moving into a new house. Now ask yourself what is the opposite of your theme? Gratitude, freezing darkness, a departure? What are the bridges between these opposites, so that both are true at the same time?

For example, you might write a story about the intense envy you feel when your best friend wins a million dollar lotto ticket. Let your words unfurl the momentous upheavals and personal disasters that the winnings create in your friend's life, which inspires gratitude for your modest means… Or you might describe a balmy summer afternoon seen through the eyes of a cold-hearted, dark-spirited, wintry CEO.

How wonderful that we have met with a paradox. Now we have some hope of making progress. –Niels Bohr

Daily Happinesses

sipping ouzo in the shade at a Greek taverna
requited love
castles in Wales
a walk in the woods
talking with a stranger on a plane
turning over a mossy rock and seeing lots of busy ants
walking through the rain at dusk

About the Author

Winslow Eliot's novels have been translated into eleven languages and published in twenty countries. She is the author of PURSUED, A PERFECT GEM, HEAVEN FALLS, and THE HAPPINESS CURE (Telemachus Press), as well as BRIGHT FACE OF DANGER (St. Martin's Press 1993 and reissued by Telemachus Press in 2010). BRIGHT FACE OF DANGER is also available in France as L'INNOCENCE DU MAL (Mira Books and Harlequin Bestsellers 2009).

Other books include WHAT WOULD YOU DO IF THERE WAS NOTHING YOU HAD TO DO? and POEMS FROM THE OASIS. She co-founded the celebrated Saturn Series Weekly Poetry Readings in New

York City, begun in 1995. Her WRITESPA—OASIS FOR WRITERS welcomes visitors from all over the world (visit her website to sign up—it's free.)The author of numerous articles, she has been a contributing author to Area, the Oriental Rug Magazine for many years, and was a reader for the Independent Film Project in New York City.

She also enjoys her work as a humanities teacher at a Waldorf high school, where she teaches seminars on poetry, literature, journalism, and creative writing.

Visit her website: http://www.winsloweliot.com

Find Out More . . .

Books by Winslow Eliot

Heaven Falls
Bright Face of Danger
A Perfect Gem
Pursued
The Happiness Cure
(Published by Telemachus Press)

The Bright Face of Danger
(St. Martin's Press 1993)
Reissued in France as *L'Innocence du Mal*
(Mira Books 2009)
Illustrated Atlas of Native American History (Saraband 1999)
ed. Samuel W. Crompton. Contributing Author: *Accommodation, Exchange, and Warfare 1600 – 1700*
The Waldorf Book of Breads (Steinerbooks 2009)
The Quest – Stories for Young Readers (Telemachus 2012)
Compiled and introduced; ed. Samantha Stier
What Would You Do If There Was Nothing You Had To Do? (Writespa 2012)
Poems from the Oasis (Writespa 2012)

By Ellie Winslow *(pen name)*:

Roman Candles (Signet/NAL 1987)
A Distant Light (Signet/NAL 1986)
Red Sky At Night (Signet/NAL 1985)
Painted Secrets (Signet/NAL 1984)
The Wine-Dark Sea (Signet/NAL 1983)

Made in the USA
Lexington, KY
20 April 2014